THEMES IN CONTEMPORARY POLICING

Themes in Contemporary Policing

Collated and edited by

William Saulsbury, Joy Mott & Tim Newburn

ISBN 0 947692 41 X

A CIP catalogue record of this book is available from the British Library.

*Information about the Independent Inquiry
and copies of its Final Report are available from:*

The Secretary
Independent Committee of Inquiry into the Role
and Responsibilities of the Police
1 Glyn Street
Vauxhall
London SE11 5RA

Tel. 0171 - 582 3744
Fax. 0171 - 587 0671

Laserset by Policy Studies Institute
Printed in Great Britain by Latimer Trend & Co Ltd, Plymouth

Contents

Contributors

David H. Bayley, Professor of Criminology, School of Criminal Justice, State University of New York at Albany, USA

Anthony Bottoms, Wolfson Professor of Criminology and Director of the Institute of Criminology, University of Cambridge

Nigel Fielding, Professor of Sociology, Deputy Dean of Human Studies, University of Surrey

Michael Hough, Professor of Social Policy, South Bank University, London

Trevor Jones, Research Fellow, Policy Studies Institute, London

Tim Newburn, Head of Crime, Justice and Youth Studies, Policy Studies Institute, London

Ken Pease, Professor of Criminology, University of Huddersfield

Clifford Shearing, Professor of Criminology, Centre of Criminology, University of Toronto, Canada

Wesley G. Skogan, Professor of Political Science and Urban Affairs, Northwestern University, Evanston, Illinois, USA

David J. Smith, Professor of Criminology, University of Edinburgh

Paul Wiles, Professor of Criminology and Dean of the Faculty of Law, University of Sheffield

Foreword

Although calls for a Royal Commission on the Police have been staunchly resisted throughout the 1980s and 1990s, the police have nevertheless been subject to intense official scrutiny. During 1993 three quite separate reviews of policing – the Royal Commission on Criminal Justice, the Sheehy Inquiry into Police Responsibilities and Rewards, and the Home Office review which led to the White Paper on Police Reform – all reported within a week of each other.

It might be thought that any further investigation would be unnecessary. However, all these major inquiries have assumed that there is consensus about the role and responsibilities of the police. In fact, such a consensus does not exist and, in describing the role of the police, these various inquiries actually contradict one another. Furthermore, what may still add up to the most far-reaching overhaul of British policing is largely taking place without major public debate.

In an attempt to stimulate such public debate on the fundamental questions and exploit the stock of knowledge that has developed over the past twenty years, the Policy Studies Institute and the Police Foundation took the step of setting up an independent committee to review the role and responsibilities of the police. The committee had a broad-based membership including senior members of the police service, academics, legal experts, representatives from the private sector and from local government. It was chaired by Sir John Cassels, Director of the National Commission on Education.

In order to inform its deliberations the committee invited some of the leading scholars in the field to prepare short papers summarising their own and others thinking on key issues affecting contemporary policing. These papers, edited for publication, are collected here. They cover a broad spectrum of subjects from crime and social trends, public opinion and police, and police patrol to private policing and crime prevention. This is a wide-ranging and provocative collection of papers which will be of considerable interest to all who are concerned about the future of policing.

Acknowledgements

This collection of papers would not have been possible without the generous financial support for the Independent Committee of Inquiry into the Role and Responsibilities of the Police provided by the Nuffield Foundation, the Esmee Fairbairn Charitable Trust, the Baring Foundation and the Dulverton Trust. In addition, we are grateful to Karin Erskine for her considerable efforts under difficult circumstances in preparing the manuscript for publication.

Explaining Crime Trends

David J. Smith

Summary

- Broadly speaking, the amount of crime recorded by the police in England and Wales increased tenfold between 1950 and 1993.

- For comparable offences the British Crime Surveys confirmed a rise in crime between 1981 and 1993.

- Most other countries with developed economies, with the exception of Japan, have experienced increases in recorded crime since 1950.

- In developed countries economic growth, with the increase in the availability of consumer goods and opportunities for theft, is far more likely than economic deprivation to account for the very marked rises in acquisitive crime.

- It is likely that social developments in Western countries since 1950 have tended to reduce the social controls and social bonding which inhibit most people from committing offences.

- Lengthy periods of high unemployment, by breaking an important social bond, may create a group of young people who are more likely to commit offences.

Introduction

In 1979 the incoming Conservative government undertook to spend 'more on fighting crime while we economise elsewhere'.[1] That pledge was a signal for the sharpening of public debate. For 30-odd years, a tacit consensus had allowed successive Home Secretaries to pursue 'progressive' policies, such as those designed to divert offenders from custody. In the face of the continued, steep rise in the rate of recorded crime, the parties have since 1979 abandoned consensus; instead they compete to come up with crime-fighting proposals with immediate appeal to voters, such as the proposed special units for the detention of persistent young offenders.

Unfortunately, the quality of this sharper public debate about rising crime has been low. Conservatives claim that catching more criminals and punishing them more severely will reduce crime. The Labour Party responds that increased crime is the product of unemployment and poverty created by the Conservatives. Neither claim is convincing in the light of the available evidence. In order to move the discussion forward, we need to take a cool look at long-term crime trends both in Britain and in other countries with advanced economies.

Crime trends in England and Wales

Substantial problems arise in compiling a time series of the statistics of 'notifiable' offences (the more serious offences) recorded by the police since 1950 in England and Wales. There have been changes in the law which introduced new offences or re-defined existing offences. In 1980 the method of compiling the statistics was changed. Over the years the figures will also have been affected by some unknown amount by changes in the extent to which victims report crimes to the police and by changes in police recording practice. Criminal Statistics England and Wales 1993 show the rates of recorded offences per 100,000 of the population between 1950 and 1993. In compiling the series, adjustments were made to take account, as far as possible, of changes in legislation so as to provide a broad picture of the extent of crime during the period.

Figure 1 shows that the rate of offences recorded by the police in England and Wales rose from around 1 per 100 of the population in 1950 to 10 per 100 in 1993, a tenfold increase. The strong upward trend began in 1955 and remained steady for the two decades up to 1975. There was some levelling off in the late 1970s, and again in the late 1980s, but each time the upward trend continued after a pause. Rising rates of recorded crime are therefore a feature of the whole post-war period; in this respect the last 15 years of Conservative government have been typical, not unusual. The increases for certain kinds of offence were much greater still. Figure 1 also shows a 28-fold increase between 1950 and 1993 in motor vehicle theft and unauthorised taking and driving away a motor vehicle without the consent of

**Figure 1   Rates of notifiable offences recorded by the police,
England and Wales 1950-1993**

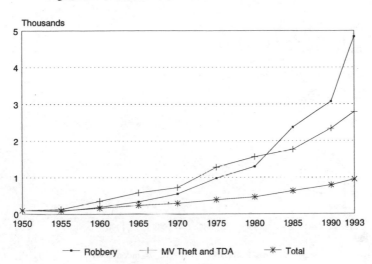

Notes

1   Rates per 100,000 population are indexed so that 1950 = 100.

2   'MV theft + TDA' = theft of motor vehicles and taking and driving away a motor
vehicle without the consent of the owner.

Source: *Criminal Statistics England and Wales*

the owner (TDA), and a 48-fold increase in robbery. These offences are
less affected than others, such as theft and burglary, by changing
definitions.

From 1981 onwards, the British Crime Survey (BCS) provides an
alternative to the statistics of crime recorded by the police.[2,3] Because
the BCS is a survey of people living in private households, it misses out
some categories of crime, such as burglaries of business premises, that
are included in the police statistics. Overall, for comparable offences,
the BCS estimated there were many more incidents than shown by
police records. In fact, because of incomplete reporting and recording,
only an estimated 27 per cent of comparable BCS crimes in 1993 ended
up in police records.[3]

Can we be sure that the upward trend in the highly incomplete
statistics of recorded crime reflects an increase in the real world? In fact

3

Figure 2 **Trends in crime, England and Wales 1981-1993: BCS and crimes recorded by the police for comparable crimes**

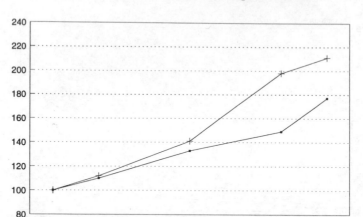

Notes

1   Two-thirds of BCS offences fall into types which can be compared with the number of crimes recorded by the police.

2   Both sets of numbers are indexed so that 1981 = 100.

Source: *Trends in Crime: Findings from the 1994 British Crime Survey*. Home Office Research and Statistics Department Research Findings No. 14

we can, because the BCS, like the recorded crime statistics, shows a strong upward trend between 1981 and 1993 for all comparable offences as shown in Figure 2. In the ten years from 1981, the rise in crime shown by the BCS was gentler than that shown by the police statistics, but was still strongly upwards. Between 1991 and 1993 this contrast was reversed, so that the BCS showed a sharper upward trend than the statistics of recorded crime. Over the whole period from 1981 to 1993, recorded crimes rose by 111 per cent, whereas BCS crimes rose by 77 per cent. The difference arises partly because of an increase in the proportion of BCS offences that were reported to the police. The statistics of recorded crime therefore exaggerated the upward trend in crime between 1981 and 1991; nevertheless, the BCS confirms that there was a very substantial increase over that period.

Figure 3 Trends in acquisitive crime, England and Wales 1981-1993: BCS and crimes recorded by the police for comparable crimes

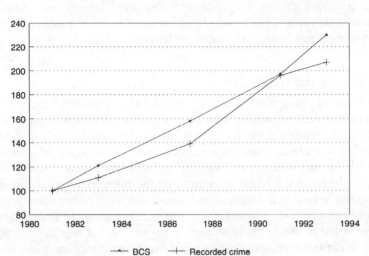

Note: Both sets of numbers are indexed so that 1981 = 100.

Source: *Trends in Crime: Findings from the 1994 British Crime Survey.* Home Office Research and Statistics Department Research Findings No. 14

Both sources show that acquisitive crimes more than doubled between 1981 and 1993 as shown in Figure 3. Within this category, there have been large increases both in vehicle thefts and in burglary, combined with particularly large increases in attempts.

For vandalism and violence, the two sources show widely divergent trends, mainly because of changes in reporting behaviour. The BCS findings provide the more realistic assessment. They showed no increase in vandalism from 1981 to 1991, followed by a sharp increase over the next two years. In 1991 only 27 per cent of BCS vandalism offences were reported to the police, with an estimated 15 per cent recorded by the police, indicating that the trend shown by police statistics is highly sensitive to changes in reporting behaviour and is plainly misleading for this kind of offence. The BCS showed a considerable increase in violent crimes between 1983 and 1993, although this upward trend was much less marked than for acquisitive crimes.

Crime surveys in the USA (from 1970) and in a number of other countries (starting more recently) have reinforced the conclusion that rises in crime shown by police statistics were largely real. Almost certainly, this also applies to the large increases in crime recorded in the post-war period before crime surveys began.

Cross-national trends

The trend of rising crime shown in England and Wales since the Second World War was repeated in most other countries with advanced economies. Since crime surveys have been introduced only recently and only in a few countries, cross-national comparisons have to rely on the recorded crime statistics collected by INTERPOL. Figure 4 shows that the rise in recorded crime in France and the Netherlands was broadly comparable to that in England and Wales, although rather less steep in France. In a later-developing European nation such as Spain, the level of recorded crime in the immediate post-war period was much lower than in earlier-developing nations, but there were large increases from the 1970s onwards. In the USA, unlike England and Wales and other European countries, the trend of rising crime levelled off in the 1980s. Most remarkably, recorded crime in Japan has remained steady over the whole post-war period. In 1951, crime was at about the same level in Japan as in other advanced nations, but by 1990 it was far lower in Japan than elsewhere because of the steep rises that had happened in other countries. Figure 4 shows only a few examples, but crime statistics for other advanced nations in the post-war period also showed a strong upward trend. Japan is the only major exception.

Figures 5 and 6 illustrate the cross-national trends for 'theft with aggravating circumstances' (such as armed robbery and breaking and entering) and for 'other' theft. The upward trends for these more specific offences are essentially the same as for all recorded offences, and Japan remains the exception.

The same Interpol statistics also show that crimes of violence other than homicide have increased substantially in most developed countries since 1977. (Comparable data on violent offences are not available for the period before 1977.) Although there were increases in homicide rates between 1951 and 1990 in a number of countries, these were generally less marked than the increases in other types of crime. England and Wales was among the half dozen countries showing no increase in homicide rate, whereas Japan showed a substantial and consistent

Figure 4　International comparisons: rates for all offences recorded by
the police 1951-1990 in England and Wales, France, Japan,
the Netherlands, Spain and the USA

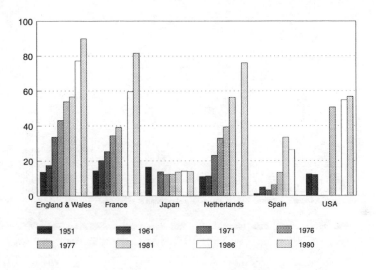

Note:　Rates per 1,000 population.

Source:　Interpol

decline. In the USA the homicide rate has risen substantially in the
post-war period, and stands at a level ten times as high as in England
and Wales or the Netherlands, the two European countries with the
lowest rates. These contrasts become even more stark when deaths by
homicide of young people are considered. World Health Organisation
statistics show that in 1987-90, annual deaths by homicide of people
aged 15 to 24 were 15.3 per 100,000 in the USA, compared with 0.9
in both the UK and the Netherlands, 0.7 in France, and 0.4 in Japan.[4]

Europeans tend to assume that the rate of crime is exceptionally high
in the USA. The recorded crime statistics suggest that this is not the case
across the USA as a whole, although there are areas of exceptionally
high crime within most US cities. On the other hand, the rate of
homicide is indeed far higher in the USA than in Europe.

Figure 5   International comparisons: rates for offences of aggravated theft
            recorded by the police 1951-1990 in England and Wales, France,
            Japan, the Netherlands, Spain and the USA

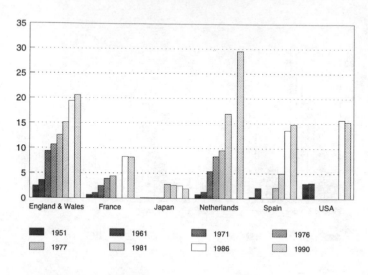

Note: Rates per 1,000 population.

Source: Interpol

Explaining trends in crime

Economic growth, unemployment, and deprivation

Most commentators assume that rising crime in developed countries is
caused by economic deprivation: by poverty, bad housing, and unemployment. At best, this 'obvious truth' is only one small part of a larger
picture. There is a contrast between the causes of crime in the individual
and the causes of the increase in the total amount of crime. Certainly,
economic deprivation goes some way towards explaining why this
person rather than that becomes a repeat offender. For example, people
on lower incomes and those living in deprived areas are more likely to
offend than people on higher incomes and those living in privileged
areas.[5] Again, unemployed people are far more likely to be arrested by
the police, and to be subsequently convicted, than those in work.[6] Yet
the period between 1950 and 1973 was a 'golden age' of economic

Figure 6 International comparisons: rates for offences of thefts recorded by the police 1951-1990 in England and Wales, France, Japan, the Netherlands, Spain and the USA

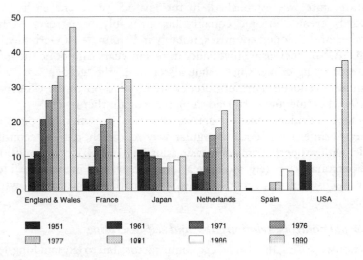

Notes
1   Rates per 1,000 population.
2   Excludes aggravated theft.

Source: Interpol

growth when unemployment remained low, standards of living increased, and the proportion of people in poverty declined; and it was also a period of rapid growth in recorded crime.

This shows that the explanations for trends in the total amount of crime are different from the explanations for the paths in life taken by individuals. *Relative* deprivation may help to explain the choices of individuals (and may also explain the way they are treated by others, and by the criminal justice system). But the overall rise in crime can certainly not be explained by economic deprivation. Indeed, that is the one explanation that can most firmly be ruled out. It is far more likely that economic *growth* has led to an increase in crime, since growth means there are more things to steal.

In the broad sweep of history, economic development tends to go along with a narrowing of the gap between the rich and the poor.[7] In the 'golden age', 1950-1973, there was probably a shift towards greater income equality in developed countries at the time when crime began to rise. In Britain this was, of course, the period when the post-war welfare state was established. In the last 15 years, the earlier shift towards greater income equality has probably been reversed in a number of developed countries, notably in Britain, West Germany, and the USA.[8] Yet increasing inequality in recent years cannot be the major cause of rising crime, since crime also rose in the 'golden age', when inequality reduced. Furthermore, crime levelled off in the USA in the 1980s when inequality started to increase again there.

There is evidence that the pattern of annual growth in property and violent crime is related in a regular way to the short-term economic cycle, with property crime decreasing during periods of economic boom and personal crime (e.g. violence against the person) increasing.[9] However, such economic trends cannot explain the long-term growth in crime.

Informal controls, relationships, and self-discipline

It is not surprising that broad economic factors fail to explain long-term crime trends. The explanation must lie in the social processes through which deviant behaviour is controlled. It is obvious that there is no simple relationship between economic structures or prosperity and the effectiveness of these controls. Not all poor or highly unequal societies are chaotic and crime-ridden, to the contrary, many are highly conformist. Nor are all rich societies crime-ridden: the exception of Japan is crucially important.

It is equally mistaken to assume that the formal legal system constitutes the main means of controlling crime. The difficult thing to explain is why most people do not commit crimes most of the time, even though the chances of apprehension and conviction would often be slight. The answer lies in informal sanctions by family, school, employer, neighbours, and even strangers. Some of these, particularly family and school, are important as agents of socialisation: the process whereby rules and values are internalised, become part of a person's outlook, and form the nucleus of a system of self-evaluation and self-discipline.[10]

In general, what restrains people from breaking informal rules, and from breaking the law, is the investment they have made in other people and institutions. There is good evidence that people who form strong and stable relationships with family, school or workplace, are less likely to offend. That is because law-breaking would threaten the relationships in which they have invested; because their behaviour is scrutinised and informally checked; and because investment in relationships and the informal controls they impose tend to create self-awareness and self-discipline.[11]

Of course, living conditions, including poverty, unemployment, and bad housing, are parts of the framework within which these social bonds are tied and untied. They probably do not influence law-breaking immediately and directly, but in the long run they may well influence the social bonding that tends to prevent law-breaking. For example, there is evidence that finding a steady job is a crucial step towards giving up a criminal career. Although the overall amount of crime does not vary in a regular way with the overall amount of unemployment, a long period of unemployment may create a group of young people who have never had a 'proper' job and expect never to get one. That long-term detachment from the labour market breaks an important social bond, and that in turn could eventually lead to an increase in crime and disorder.

Urban ways of life

Throughout the world crime is much higher in large towns than in villages, probably because in towns the populations are more heterogeneous and mobile, people observe each other less, and social relationships are less constraining. Yet increasing urbanisation cannot account for rising crime in Britain in the post-war period, since the population was tending to spread out rather than concentrate further at that time. However, there is evidence that crime rates are high in specific urban areas where social controls have tended to break down, and that sudden changes in the local population and in how land and buildings are used can precipitate a shift to a high local rate of crime.[12]

Families

There is a large body of evidence to show that badly functioning families tend to produce children who break the law. Where the parents are in conflict, where they neglect or fail to supervise the children, reject them, or use harsh or erratic discipline, the children tend to develop a range of problem behaviours, including crime.[13] Major changes in family structure have taken place in the post-war period, including large increases in the rate of divorce, the number of single parents, and cohabiting as an alternative to marriage.[14] Whether these changes in family structure have led to an increase in family conflict and bad parenting is not known. A decline in the quality of parenting *may* be among the explanations for the rise in crime, but further evidence is needed on this important point. Because the changes in family structures are comparatively recent and swift-moving, up-to-date information is needed.

Opportunity

It has been convincingly argued that offending arises from an interaction between the individual and a constellation of competing risks and rewards. Many factors may influence the risks and rewards and the way the offender perceives them. These include the design of buildings, the layout of streets, shopping centres, entertainment areas; the amount and nature of goods available to be stolen; how business is organised (for example, whether payments are made by cash, by cheque, or by credit card); and the pattern of people's daily habits and activities. There is a large body of evidence to show that specific crimes can be prevented by reducing the opportunities for them to occur.[15] It is likely that at least part of the post-war rise in crime has occurred because opportunities have increased. For example, motor vehicle crime accounted for one-quarter of BCS offences in 1991, whereas in the immediate post-war period these offences were small in number because of the far smaller number of motor vehicles in use at that time.

Law enforcement

Studies that follow individuals over a long period have shown that those who are convicted, and especially those who are sent to prison, become more likely to re-offend as a result.[16] The underlying reasons are that punishment tends to be degrading rather than uplifting, and that the effect of sanctions is to loosen the offender's social bonds with law-abiding people and normal institutions. Yet presumably the actual chance of conviction has some influence on the decision-making of people who might be tempted to offend. These two effects counteract each other, but we know little or nothing about the balance between them.

In countries with high crime rates, only a small proportion of offences are detected: in England and Wales, for example, only 3 per cent of BCS offences are estimated to lead to a caution or conviction.[17] However, it has not been demonstrated that increasing the rate of detection and conviction reduces crime. It is in principle possible that the post-war rise in crime was caused by a decline in the rate of detection and conviction, but it is likely that, instead, the rise in crime caused a decline in the detection rate.

Conclusions

Changes in informal social controls and social bonds must lie at the heart of any explanation of the remarkable post-war increase in crime in countries with developed economies. In line with that view, Japan, where the rate of crime has remained low, is characterised by closely-knit and interlocking social and institutional relationships. It is likely that a range of social developments in the West have tended to reduce informal controls and to weaken social bonding. More specific factors that *may* be causes of the rise in crime are family conflict and inadequate parenting, increasing mobility, declines in the cohesiveness of local communities, and changes in the pattern of crime opportunities and risks. It seems clear that poverty and inadequate housing are not in themselves causes of rising crime, although they may influence factors (such as family life) that in turn have an influence on crime.

Unstable attachment to employment is certainly a link in the chain of development leading the individual to re-offend, but changes in the total amount of unemployment are not related in a regular way with changes in the total amount of crime. It remains possible that a lengthy period of high unemployment will create new conditions in which a section of the population becomes detached from the labour market and from the social fabric, and that crime will rise rapidly among that group.

In part the post-war rise in crime probably arises from an increase in opportunity for theft. Thus, economic growth and the large increase in the quantity of consumer goods *may* be among the causes of the rise in crime.

References

1. Conservative Party. (1979) *Manifesto*. London: Conservative Party.
2. Mayhew, P., Aye Maung N. and Mirrlees-Black C. (1993) *The 1992 British Crime Survey*. Home Office Research Study No. 132. London: HMSO.
3. Mayhew, P., Mirrlees-Black C. and Aye Maung N. (1995) *Trends in crime: Findings from the 1994 British Crime Survey*. Research Findings No. 14. London: Home Office Research and Statistics Department.
4. UNICEF (1993) *The Progress of Nations 1993*. New York: UNICEF.

5. Braithwaite, J. (1981) The myth of social class and criminality reconsidered. *American Sociological Review,* 46, pp 36-57.

6. Smith, D.J. (1983) *Police and People in London Vol 1: A Survey of Londoners.* London: Policy Studies Institute.

7. Smith, D.J. (1995) Living conditions in the twentieth century. In Rutter, M. and Smith, D.J. (eds) *Psychosocial Disorders in Young People: Time Trends and Their Causes.* Chichester: Wiley.

8. Green, G., Coder, J. and Ryscavage, P. (1990) *International Comparisons of Earnings Inequality for Men in the 1980s.* Luxembourg: Luxembourg Income Study Working Paper 58.

9. Field, S. (1990) *Trends in Crime and Their Interpretation: A Study of Recorded Crime in Post-war England and Wales.* Home Office Research Study No. 119. London: HMSO.

10. Bandura, A. (1991) Social cognitive theory of moral thought and action. In Kurtines, W.M. and Gewirtz, J.L. (eds) *Handbook of Moral Behavior and Development. Volume I: Theory.* Hillsdale, NJ: Lawrence Erlbaum.

11. Sampson, R.J. and Laub, J.H. (1993) *Crime in the Making: Pathways and Turning Points through Life.* Cambridge, MA/London: Harvard University Press.

12. Schuerman, L. and Kobrin, S. (1986) Community careers in crime. In Reiss A.J. Jnr and Tonry, M. (eds) *Communities and Crime.* Chicago: University of Chicago Press.

13. Loeber, R. and Stouthamer-Loeber, M. (1986) Family factors as correlates and predictors of juvenile conduct problems and delinquency. In Tonry, M. and Morris, N. (eds) *Crime and Justice: an Annual Review of Research.* Volume 7. Chicago: University of Chicago Press.

14. Hess, L. (1995) Changing family patterns in Western Europe: opportunity and risk factors for adolescent development. In Rutter, M. and Smith, D.J. (eds) *Psychosocial Disorders in Young People: Time Trends and Their Causes.* Chichester: Wiley.

15. Clarke, R.V.G. (ed) (1992) *Situational Crime Prevention: Successful Case Studies.* New York: Harrow and Weston.

16. Farrington, D.P. (1977) The effects of public labelling. *British Journal of Criminology,* 17, pp 112-125.
    Farrington, D.P., Osborn, S.G. and West, D.J. (1978) The persistence of labelling effects. *British Journal of Criminology,* 18, pp 277-284.

17. Barclay, G. (ed) (1993) *Digest 2: Information on the Criminal Justice System in England and Wales.* London: Home Office Research and Statistics Department.

Crime and Policing in a Changing Social Context

Anthony Bottoms and *Paul Wiles*

Summary

- The social geography and the crime maps of the contemporary city have changed as the result of the demands of international capital and business and changes in the production process.

- Developments in economics and in communication and transport technology have created a global metropolitan culture and consumer market that offers a wide range of choices of self-identify and life-styles which those without money can only acquire by illegal means.

- As the highest income earners earn more and the lowest earners proportionately less, a disadvantaged 'underclass' may emerge which might either result in an increase in crime in the city or develop into a culture of hopelessness.

- The decline of traditional group affiliations in Western societies could be associated with an increase in crime, and with demands for harsher forms of social controls.

- Widespread use of technical control devices to prevent crime may increase individual feelings of security but may be most successful in reducing the less visible forms of crime such as fraud.

- The resources of the public police in Britain are being stretched by trying to respond to a wide range of both international and specialised local control needs.

- With an increasing tendency for the social world to be perceived as a series of private realms and interests which take responsibility for dealing with their own problems the role of the public police is being undermined by the growth of private policing.

- Increased international travel and tourism has resulted in the development of facilities that are international in style and provide secured, protected and normalised environments which are becoming the model for 'defended locales' in all cities.

- A strategy of social control for cities based on a series of private defended locales from which those who are no longer needed are excluded is fragile because it will only be effective until the defences are breached.

Introduction

It hardly seems likely that the increases in crime over the last 40 years are simply the product of traditional urbanism – not least since most Western countries, while indeed becoming more urban in the post-war period, have done so at a rate much slower than the increase in crime. It is possible that we need to dig more deeply into issues of contemporary social change if we are to understand adequately the nature of crime at the present time, why it has increased, likely future changes in crime levels and patterns, and the changing nature of social control, including policing. This paper considers some important economic and social developments in contemporary societies, particularly in Britain, and the ways in which they are relevant to aspects of crime in the city.

The changing nature of cities

Internationalisation of capital and business

Developments in the nature of capital and business have created multi-national corporations whose day-to-day operations can often transcend national boundaries. Capital can now be moved so easily and rapidly round the world that it is no longer possible for governments to control or direct its flows, and the power of effective decision has in many instances been removed from the nation state. International capital will seek to invest, and multi-national corporations to develop, where they believe profit can be maximised regardless of the needs or policies of regions or nation states, and they are no longer constrained as they once were by, for example, the location of raw material, or difficulties in transport. Thus, the location for economic activity has become much more a matter of corporate choice rather than geographical necessity.

There are some cities which have become major locations for the transferring and brokering of international capital and financial services, for example, New York, London and Tokyo, which will be reflected in their crime patterns. Because major building developments in the city now usually involve international capital the result is the growth of the 'international city', with growing homogenisation in architecture and design and this will also effect patterns of crime and the measures of social control adopted.

Politics and city development

Some of the factors which reduce the autonomy of the nation state will equally, and almost certainly, affect the local state. The local state will, for example, find it even more difficult than the nation-state to resist the power of international capital and corporations. An example of this is the local state's control over the planning of the built environment which is likely to be legally strengthened since technological capability needs to be integrated and planned. Nevertheless, there may well be occasions when planning controls are believed to be inhibiting large-scale new development and, in Britain at least, devices have often been found to bypass the normal planning processes and the political interests of the local state.

A further political development in Britain concerns welfare provision. In the post-war period especially, the local state has been responsible for the provision of many services ranging from education and social services to housing and these, especially the latter, have changed the crime maps of post-war Britain. The growing fiscal costs, allied to an ideology of elective choice, are now threatening universal welfare provision and the local state will be left to deal with the consequences.

Counteracting these concerns has been the development of enshrined human rights at a supra-national level – so that even a country like Britain which had no such constitutional rights, has now received them under the European Convention. In theory such rights act to protect groups threatened by exclusion. However, this may not always be the case. For example, traditional rights of universal access to public space may be threatened by the increasing development of so-called 'mass private property' (i.e. land in private ownership which is accessible to a mass audience, such as shopping malls and leisure complexes) or, more generally, such rights could become purely formal and procedural and devoid of any real content.

Changes in the production process

In most developed economies the general trend has been for a reduction in the demand for the products of heavy industry, with employment in such industries declining, leaving behind 'rustbelt cities' with decaying landscapes and outdated social structures. Production has become increasingly automated and less labour intensive and on a smaller scale, with a move to new 'green field' sites or to 'sunrise cities' where living conditions are pleasant and costs often lower.

For cities which have traditionally been dependent on heavy manufacturing industry the closure of plants and factories, and the shifting of those that remain away from traditional locations, have left large derelict areas. This may create conditions of urban blight and the depression of the abandoned inner city, or it may provide locations for the major re-modelling of the commercial geography with the development of large shopping and leisure complexes. The decline and/or relocation of manufacturing can leave some poorer residential areas, originally built for the workers, isolated from possible sources of employment.

These changes in the processes of production will produce different crime outcomes in cities from those of the past.

The city and its hinterland

The idea of the city as a defined geographical area with clear boundaries and a specific economically-related hinterland has been eroded. The movement of population beyond the suburbs into the surrounding countryside means that the hinterland may spread up to fifty miles beyond the city. The decay of the traditional inner city, as new locations for shopping, entertainment and employment emerge around the city, can create in extreme cases, a 'doughnut effect', with a ring of satellite dormitory towns around the city which is left with a hollow core. The emergence of functionally differentiated areas within and around the city means that people move across and between these areas rather than simply in and out of the city.

For crime, this broadening of the city has some important consequences. First, if the city begins to hollow out there is a danger that the lowest social groups will remain trapped in the hollowed-out core creating ideal conditions for ghettoisation. Second, since up to now the most criminogenic groups of young males in cities have not travelled great distances, the result will increasingly be impacted criminal areas with multiple victimisation and offending.[1] Third, the most attractive

18

targets for property crime will be in the suburbs or the rural hinterland, attracting more socially confident and experienced criminals. It is these last two factors, taken together, which possibly explain why urban/rural crime differences have narrowed in recent years, but not to the extent one might expect.

Effects of technology

Giddens[2] has noted that one of the crucial features of contemporary society is 'time/space distanciation' – the 'stretching of social systems across time and space' – following developments in communication and transport technology. The patterning of daily social life and social events are, as a result, much less dependent upon local traditions and cultures, they are just as likely to be influenced by what is happening far away in space and time as nearby (for example, the internationalisation of aspects of youth culture and dress.)

Time/space distanciation has implications for the city and for crime in the city. First, all cities are now part of a global metropolitan culture, embracing a kaleidoscope of images and styles with increasingly little connection with local conditions and from which we can pick and choose. Self-identity in such a world is obviously to some extent elective. The cultural kaleidoscope is largely a consumer market so that without money many of the choices offered are not available, or at least, not available legally. To deny self-identity to those without money makes it almost inevitable that at least some will seek such identities through deviant means.

Second, the relativity of modern culture, and the assumption of choice, makes it increasingly difficult for individual nation states clearly to define and reinforce the outer boundaries they wish to maintain for their cultural and legal systems. Whilst this is unlikely to affect core values and legal rules (for example, prohibitions against assault or burglary) it is certainly likely to affect the periphery, especially where there are pre-existing differences between nation states who are participants in the same global culture (for example, in drug use prohibitions). Such confusions could weaken the capacity of social control both in terms of internalised norms and of public reactions to deviance.

The search for security

Giddens[3] has also argued that our reliance on abstract systems created by time/space distanciation means that social life becomes dependent on acquired knowledge rather than tradition. As knowledge becomes ever more specialised, we increasingly have simply to put our trust in the expertise of others and in abstract systems. The combination of the fragmentation of the city together with the inevitable risk-taking of modern life, it can be argued, creates a new problem of personal security.

Insecurity can be dealt with by creating environments of trust which either display the authority of expertise, or technological competence, or which calm doubts and insecurities. These aspects are to be found in modern crime control systems: the displays of police technology to persuade us of detective expertise and the closed circuit television (CCTV) cameras in the streets to reassure us that we are guarded. In the city we see an increasing emphasis on creating such environments of trust. Calming insecurity and creating trust is, however, different from security as such. Security devices may create some trust, but they may also heighten feelings of insecurity by suggesting there is some threat to be guarded against.

New forms of social differentiation

Gender

Two aspects of changes in the production process have tended to lead to an increase in the number of females in the labour force. The general decline in manufacturing industry, and especially the decline in skilled and semi-skilled jobs in such industries, has eroded the supply of traditionally male jobs. The increase in service industries has especially created jobs which in many cultures are seen as female occupations, or has created part-time jobs that are disproportionately filled by females.

This change has produced different patterns of routine activities which may have an indirect effect on the crime rate, for example, if more houses are left empty during the day the opportunities for burglary increase.[4] Less straightforwardly, but also potentially of considerable importance, it is likely that these changes will have subtle effects on within-family relationships and the socialisation of children, reinforced by changes in attitudes to marriage. The precise effects will depend on cultural differences but might, in countries with greater economic and political emancipation of women, include both an increase in the divorce rate and an increase in the reporting of domestic violence as a crime. It is noteworthy that the conviction rates for women in England have been increasing at a greater rate than those for men over the last 20 years.

Economic polarisation

There seems to be a tendency over time in many societies for the highest group of income earners to earn proportionately more of the national income and for the lowest group to earn less.[5] Among the reasons for this are the growth of structural unemployment; an aging population; the growth of part-time jobs in the service sector, especially when the only wage-earner in the household is so employed; technological replacement of traditional middle-income skills; high rewards for some managers; the tendency of some governments, in an increasingly consumer-oriented context, to switch from direct to indirect taxation and to reduce the upper rates of income tax but without corresponding increases in welfare benefits for the poor.

Income polarisation creates a new respectable poor but they, like the old respectable poor, are not of much criminological interest. However, it also creates a new particularly disadvantaged group which is in danger of becoming an 'underclass' which is effectively excluded from the membership of civil society.[6] In the United States there is a tendency to assume that such an underclass is necessarily associated with, and a product of, ethnic differences. Our view is that there is no such necessary connection.

The extent to which an economically disadvantaged group becomes an underclass will not entirely depend on income polarisation but also on how far the geography and social organisation of the city concentrates such groups in particular areas.[7] The effect of these factors will vary from country to country according to the nature of the national housing market, and from city to city depending on whether it has developed in such a way as to leave a hollowed-out core.

The development of an underclass has involved a significant shift in the logic of capitalism. Studies have shown that around 1900, when industry needed unskilled labour, and all males had been enfranchised politically, there was a tendency for those in power to create mechanisms of social inclusion, such as social insurance, backed by normalizing institutions, such as education and social work.[8] Nowadays social inclusion seems to be no longer necessary either economically, because of automation and structural unemployment, or politically, because elections can be won without the votes of the most disadvantaged.

The existing criminological literature does not provide clear pointers to the likely consequences for crime of the emergence of an underclass in cities. Among the possibilities are: higher relative deprivation and higher unemployment will produce higher theft rates which, at worst, could result in organised predation of the rest of the city and the highways; if the criminal law is applied strictly it could result in an increase in criminality based on revenge; the trapping of the underclass in a ghetto could result in internally high crime and victimisation rates, but with little external predation; the development of a culture of hopelessness without, necessarily, high crime rates.[9]

Group affiliations

One slow and long-term consequence of the structural changes in the economy has been an erosion of the importance of social class as traditionally understood as an indicator of social affiliation and differentiation, and its partial replacement by 'life style'. Lifestyles are individualistic, fluid and transitory and are available to anyone who can purchase the symbols of membership on the market. They are related to consumer culture, which means they are international and susceptible to manipulation by the media.

In traditional societies group affiliations, such as kinship, local communities, religion and societal tradition are sources of trust. In contemporary Western societies sources of trust tend to be either more individualistic (based on intimate on-to-one relationships) or based on abstract systems. This change could have considerable criminological significance because of the established importance of group norms in constraining individual action. Indeed, it is the continuing strength of group norms in Japan for cultural reasons, and despite many of the modern economic and social changes, that seem to have allowed that country to maintain a low crime rate in the post-war period.[10]

In addition, it could be argued that the decline of group affiliations and solidarity (i.e. informal social control) in modern western societies means that formal social control is the remaining defence against deviance, leading to demands for more specialised and harsher forms of control when crime increases.

Youth culture

The development of a global youth culture linked to consumerism, has resulted in much teenage leisure activity being carried out in age-specific groups. Such groups tend to congregate in public spaces and may be regarded as threatening regardless of their intent. The result is adverse reactions by shopkeepers, social control agents etc. There is some evidence that this may be happening in Britain, at least when the group contains members of an ethnic minority.[11]

An important feature of the growth of the 'mass private property' of shopping malls and leisure complexes is that groups of this sort can be asked to leave with no reasons needing legally to be given, and indeed, even permanent exclusion may be ordered – it is not difficult to see this as a potential source of resentment. The owners and managers of mass private property are, however, unlikely to be influenced by any considerations of justice for a small number of excluded individuals, being more interested in the utilitarian pursuit of the greatest happiness for the greatest number and, of course, their own profit margins.

Criminological consequences of new forms of social differentiation

The changing forms of social differentiation will almost certainly interact in extremely complex ways to influence the distribution of crimes and offenders within cities and perhaps the overall national level of crime. For example, the social value of the school as an integrative and offender-preventing institution[12] may be reduced by economic polarisation, the declining importance of group ethics and the advent of elective individualism. Further, crime rates in cities are likely to vary according to the dominant values of different societies and of the nature the city within that society (traditional, sunrise, rustbelt, tourist centre etc).

Social control and the city

Technical control

One of the most obvious aspects of social control in the contemporary city, which clearly distinguishes it from earlier eras, is the use of technical control devices. These include CCTV cameras in streets, shops and car parks; automatic entry and exit devices in car parks; car alarms; varieties of burglar alarm; PIN number access systems; entryphones – the list seems endless.

Technical engineering to reduce crime has certainly been heavily invested in and the public may welcome it because it increases their sense of security. Although there are many examples of specific types of crime being prevented by technical devices,[13] the development of increasingly sophisticated technical controls against crime has gone together with a constant rise in the overall crime rate. Presumably this is because there are a greater number of other variables relevant to crime, such as the decline in group affiliations, which may have more than counteracted the successes of technical control.

The fitting of such devices is not necessarily related to systematic risk evaluation, nor is their utility always properly evaluated although the police and the insurance industry encourage their use.[14] While technical devices may not reduce the amount of crime they may influence the targeting of crime, for example, car alarms may not reduce the overall amount of car theft but only of vehicles fitted with them.

Technical control may be more successful in some areas of crime which are less visible. The ability to monitor employees' use of telephones, photocopiers, computers, the use of information systems to analyze work and business processes in search of aberrant patterns, monitor stock movement etc. may be successful in reducing some forms of white collar crime. Business has increasingly developed a series of preventive strategies to reduce crime by the use of management systems backed up by technology.[15]

Segmentation of social control

In most western societies formal social control has been dominated for over 150 years by the public police. They have never had a total monopoly and other forms of formal social control have existed in parallel, especially in business and commerce. However, there is growing empirical evidence that the dominance of the police is being undermined and questioned.

In Britain, at least, organisations ranging from groups of residents to local government authorities are setting up alternative patrolling services, frequently to patrol public streets. To an increasing extent public activities, such as shopping, transport or leisure pursuits, take place on 'mass private property' controlled by private security agencies. Many places of employment, ranging from factories to universities, have their own private police forces. As a generalisation, policing is increasingly fragmenting into forms designed to deal with the problems of policing different places or to provide policing of different functions.

The initial impetus for much of this alternative provision has been dissatisfaction with the services provided by public policing. There is a market in social control, as in any other service, and if the dominant provider ceases to be effective then new providers will enter the market if they are allowed to. The new forms of segregation and fragmentation in the contemporary city have produced very different social control needs and these, like any differentiated market, can often be most effectively responded to by dedicated, targeted services. By attempting to remain a generalist service, with the expensive and wide-ranging training of officers that this entails, the public police inevitably incurs much higher costs than specialist providers.[16]

Lying behind dissatisfaction with public policing are two broad trends. Public policing in Britain is being stretched. On the one hand, they are trying to respond to the control needs of globalisation, ranging from policing the new 'border-free' Europe to controlling fraud in the City of London's financial services. On the other hand, they are being asked to respond to increasingly localised control needs. The British state is tending to respond to these pressures by ever more centralised managerial and fiscal control over the operations of police forces (which is made simpler by modern information technology). However, this response, almost inevitably, makes it more unlikely that the police will be able to respond flexibly to differentiated and localised needs. Greater control and direction at the nation state level is only likely to increase dissatisfaction in local perceptions of public policing.

The second broad theme is a decline in the ideal of a public civic polity – what some writers have referred to as a decline of 'civil society'. In Britain this has been particularly visible in the privatisation of public services and the curtailing of the power of local government. The result has been a decline of the ideal that social problems should be identified and responded to as public matters, and that citizenship in the public realm is a central good. Increasingly the social world is perceived as a series of private realms which must take responsibility for their own problems, and where the public good is simply the market outcome of these processes. In such a framework, private interests will expect their control needs to be met on their own terms – something a public police is least equipped to do, and indeed, was partly developed to prevent.

The alternative is for private interests to satisfy their control needs through private policing and this they are doing. In Britain there are few constraints on such developments, for example, there is no licensing system for private security firms and few legal constraints on patrolling the streets. Additionally, many of our traditional legal protections against private interests being pursued though social control relate to activities in the public realm and are irrelevant to 'mass private property'. Moreover, the public/private distinction is being carefully manipulated by vested interests to achieve such control.

Another consequence of the fragmentation of control and the decline of the dominance of the public police is that social control has developed as a business. Like any other contemporary business it has become internationalised, for example, bids to run a new private prison in Britain may come from companies who already have experience of such work in France or the USA. Some commentators have even suggested that increasingly national control strategies are being determined by such companies rather than nation states.[17]

Defended locales

Increased travel for business and tourism has created the problem of how individuals ensure their safety in strange cities and countries. Facilities have been developed that are deliberately international in style so that the skills learned in one's own city of recognizing danger signs and how to gain help and safety are immediately transferable. For example, car hire firms, hotel chains and restaurants operate internationally and guarantee they will be the same everywhere. At the extreme 'tourist bubbles' can envelop travellers so that they only move inside secured, protected and normalised environments where the learned defence responses of home will still apply to everything from personal security to food.

It is important to realise that special control strategies (of the kind developed for tourists) are increasingly the model even within one's native city. As cities fragment and geographically and socially differentiate, then the needs of the traveller become the needs of us all in all cities. We are offered a wide range of choices but if that range is not to increase our insecurity it needs to be offered in a framework which is predictable, secure and known. The shopping mall may offer us a range of 'lifestyle adventures', but within a clearly protected and defended locale. The contemporary city is developing a geography in which there are a series of such defended locales.

The difficult question is whether these developments will continue to the point at which the city consists of a series of defended locales, linked by protected routes, but with 'badlands' elsewhere – the ultimate ghettoisation of everyday life. Such a development would be the final collapse of the idea of a civic polity and a return to an almost medieval notion of the public and private realm. The trends which could lead to such a nightmare can already be seen in some cities or parts of cities, or in aspects of life in the city.

One central problem with achieving social control through defended locales (quite apart from the moral or political objections) is that it is ultimately a very fragile strategy. Like the medieval walled city, a defended locale only works until the defences are breached and then it ceases to work at all. Defended locales necessarily involve excluding those who are seen as dangerous or undesirable, and the more such tactics are used to serve only private interests the more crude such exclusions may become.

Cities have always had a choice of either achieving order through the use of control or attempting to do so through legitimation. The modern technology of control and the globalisation of cities sometimes seems to offer the possibility of much easier legitimate control. However, as Galbraith[18] and others have pointed out, this is only achieved by gaining legitimation from the majority but ignoring the minority. It is this strategy which may increase the segmentation and differentiated control locales of the contemporary city. In the longer term it may contain the recipe for urban riots. Alternatively, it is possible that majority legitimation may be sufficient to maintain order, and that the excluded will retreat into a culture of hopelessness or of sporadic predation.

Conclusions

In spite of global trends in economic and social change there remain differences at the regional, national and city level in precisely how these trends affect life in a particular city. We have pointed to a possible 'doomsday scenario' in which the public realm of civil society collapses into a world of private, secured spaces from which those who are no longer needed are excluded. We do not believe that such a world will necessarily emerge, although the indications of how it could are clearly identifiable. However, if our world is to find security without such a solution then we urgently need to understand much more about the comparative and international dimensions of the development of modern cities, modern crime and modern social control.

References

1. Pease, K. (1993) Individual and community influences on victimisation and their implications for crime prevention. In Farrington, D.P., Sampson, R.J. and Wikstrom, P-O.H. (eds) *Integrating Individual and Ecological Aspects of Crime.* Stockholm: National Council for Crime Prevention.

2. Giddens, A. (1984) *The Constitution of Society.* Cambridge: Polity Press.

3. Giddens, A. (1990) *The Consequences of Modernity.* Cambridge: Polity Press.

4. Cohen, L.E. and Felson, M. (1979) Social change and crime rate trends: a routine activities approach. *American Sociological Review,* 44, pp 588-608.
   Felson, M. (1994) *Crime and Everyday Life.* California: Pine Forge Press.

5. Griffin, T. (1991) *Social Trends.* HMSO: London.

6. Murray, C. (1990) *The Emerging English Underclass.* London: Institute of Economic Affairs.

7. Wiles, P. (1992) Ghettoisation in Europe? *European Journal on Social Policy,* 1, pp 52-69.

8. Garland, D. (1985) *Punishment and Welfare.* Aldershot: Gower.

9. Rose, E.J.B. (1969) *Colour and Citizenship: A Report on English Race Relations.* London: Oxford University Press.

10. Moriyama, T. (1993) Crime, criminal justice and social control in Japan: why do we enjoy a low crime rate? *Paper presented to the British Criminology Conference.*

11. Phillips, S. and Cochrane, R. (1988) *Crime and Nuisance in the Shopping Centre.* Crime Prevention Series Paper 16. London: Home Office.

12. Graham, J. (1988) *Schools, Disruptive Behaviour and Delinquency.* Home Office Research Study No. 96. London: HMSO

13. Clarke. R.V.G. (ed) (1992) *Situational Crime Control: Successful Case Studies.* New York: Harvard and Heston.

14. Johnson, V., Shapland, J. and Wiles, P. (1994) *Crime on Industrial Estates.* Crime Prevention Series. London: Home Office.

15. Burrows, J. (1988) *Retail Crime: Prevention through Crime Analysis.* Crime Prevention Series. London: Home Office.

16. Wiles, P. (1993) Policing structures, organisational change and personnel management. In Dingwall, J. and Shapland, J. (eds) *Reforming British Policing: Missions and Structures.* University of Sheffield: Faculty of Law.

17. Moyle, P. (1993) Private contract management of correctional facilities in Queensland: a policy New Zealand should not follow.; *Paper presented to the British Criminology Conference.*

18. Galbraith, J.K. (1992) *The Culture of Contentment.* London: Sinclair Stevenson.

Summarised from the second part of a paper entitled 'Crime and Insecurity in the City' presented at a conference of the International Society of Criminology, Leuven, Belgium, 1994; to be published in the proceedings of the conference, edited by Cyrille Fijnaut.

What Do the Police Do?

David H. Bayley

Summary

- Modern police forces perform two major functions: authoritative intervention and symbolic justice. Most police officers are engaged in one or other of these most of the time.

- The purpose of authoritative intervention is to restore order. Authoritative intervention is what patrol and traffic officers are primarily responsible for. It is almost wholly reactive, rarely anticipatory. Crime is involved only occasionally or ambiguously.

- Symbolic justice is the realm of detective and traffic officers. Also largely reactive, it is achieved through law enforcement. Its purpose is demonstrative, to show offenders and public that a regime of law exists.

- What the police do is strikingly similar around the world. Among the forces in the five countries studied about 60 per cent of police personnel patrol and respond to requests from the public, 15 per cent investigate crime, 9 per cent regulate traffic and 9 per cent administer.

- Patrol work is determined entirely by what the public ask the police to do. The majority of police officers spend most of their time restoring order and providing general assistance.

- The police spend very little of their time in dealing with crime, and when they do, it is with crimes that have already been committed. Detectives know they are unlikely to be able to find the perpetrators of crimes unless they are identified by the victims or people at the scene. As a result most crime, especially property crime, goes unsolved.

- The reason the police are not preventing crime is because what they do in practice has little relation to crime or the social conditions that produce crime.

- Any systematic effect police may have in preventing crime must come through deterrence which mainly depends on the larger criminal justice system. Altogether any deterrent effect appears to be weak.

- Police forces around the world are organised to do the same sorts of work regardless of the social circumstances they confront. They do not adapt to the work they must do, rather the work they must do is adapted to the police organisation.

Introduction

The research findings described here are based on four years, from 1989 to 1993, of intensive research with 28 police forces in five countries – 7 in Australia, 3 in England and Wales, 6 in Canada, 3 in Japan and 9 the United States. The countries were chosen because they are similar politically and economically and are accessible for research on the police. Each police force studied provided information on their performance from existing records and files and it is a reflection of what police managers themselves have at hand when they make decisions about police activities. I made a special point of visiting commands where something explicitly new or experimental was taking place. Within each police force I collected information about the activities of a cross section of police stations selected from urban, suburban and rural locations. Information on police performance was collected from 12 front-line stations in Australia, 8 in England and Wales, 3 in Canada, 12 in Japan and 11 in the United States. In addition, I observed police operations in the field and interviewed police managers and supervisors at all levels.

Patrolling

Patrolling is by far the biggest assignment in policing. In the United States 65 per cent of police officers are assigned to patrol work, 64 per cent in Canada, 56 per cent in England and Wales, 54 per cent in Australia, and 40 per cent in Japan. These officers work round the clock every day of the year, in uniform, usually in marked radio patrol cars.

Patrol work is determined almost entirely by what the public ask the police to do. Contrary to what most people think, the police do not enforce their own conception of order on an unwilling populace. Almost all they do is undertaken at the request of some member of the public. If the public stopped calling the police, the police would have to re-invent their job.

Driving slowly around their assigned beats, patrol officers wait for radio dispatchers to relay calls that have come over the well-publicised emergency telephone numbers. In cities, over 90 per cent of the work of patrol officers is generated by dispatch. Self-initiated, or proactive work in police jargon, occurs more frequently in less developed or rural areas.[1]

Stopping motor vehicles that have violated traffic law accounts for the largest proportion of self-generated work, at least in Australia, Canada and the United States. Patrol officers spend the rest of their time discouraging behaviour that they view as disruptive or unseemly, such as drunks sleeping in front of doorways, teenage boys hanging around on street corners, prostitutes soliciting, or men urinating against a wall around the corner from a busy bar.

Very little of the work patrol officers do has to do with crime. British and U.S. studies have consistently shown that not more than 25 per cent of all the calls to the police are about crime, more often the figure is 15-20 per cent.[2] Moreover, what is initially reported by the public as a crime is often found not to be a crime by the police who respond.[3] For example, lonely elderly people may report burglaries in progress so that police will come and talk to them for a while. Thus, the real proportion of requests to the police that involve crime may be more like 7-10 per cent.

Most of the genuine crime the police are called upon to handle is minor. In the United States, using the categories provided by the Uniform Crime Reports, one finds that from 1984 to 1990 violent crime (homicide, forcible rape, aggravated assault, robbery) averaged 13 per cent of all reported serious crime (violent crime plus burglary, larceny theft and auto theft). In Australia violent crime accounts for about 2 per cent of reported serious crime. The ratio of reported violent to serious crime tends to be higher in large cities, but violent crime still represents only 25 per cent of the total of reported crime in New York city, 12 per cent in Houston, 26 per cent in Los Angeles, 16 per cent in Montreal and 17 per cent in Toronto.

If one compares violent crime to all crime no matter how trivial, such as minor shoplifting, disturbing the peace, vandalism, minor property theft, and so on, the proportion is much lower. In 1990 violent crimes accounted for around 1 per cent of all reported crime in Australia, 9 per cent in Canada, 5 per cent in England and Wales, and 1 per cent in Japan.

Not only is crime a minor part of patrol work and often not especially serious, the trail is almost always cold by the time the police arrive, with the culprit having been gone for hours and often days. This is typical of crimes against property, the largest category of serious crimes.

If the majority of police officers are not directly fighting crime, what are they doing? The answer is they are restoring order and providing general assistance. In the apt words of Egon Bittner[4] the key function of the police is to stop 'something that ought not to be happening and about which someone had better do something now'. Police interrupt and pacify situations of potential or ongoing conflict. Typical instances are young men drinking beer on a street corner and making rude remarks, tenants refusing to leave an apartment from which they have been evicted, a dog barking persistently late at night, a truculent and inconsiderate neighbour obstructing a driveway with his car. Most of the time the police do not use the criminal law to restore calm and order. They rarely make arrests, though the threat of doing so always exists.

When officers are called to actual or potential conflicts they try to 'sort out', as the British say, what has been going on and to produce a truce that will last until the officer gets away. Is there an offence? Who is the victim? This searching for the truth is often very difficult. People lie brazenly, which explains in large part why the police become cynical and hard to convince. Or people tell self-serving, partially true stories. The police 'sort out' situations by listening patiently to endless stories about fancied slights, old grievances, new insults, mismatched expectations, infidelity, dishonesty and abuse. They hear all about the petty, mundane, tedious, hapless, sordid details of individual lives. Patient listening and gentle counselling are undoubtedly what patrol officers do most of the time.

The most common, as well as the most difficult, conflict situations the police handle are disputes within families. Officers round the world claim that such disturbances are more common on days when public assistance cheques are delivered, because then people have the money to drink.

Research into the handling of domestic disputes in the United States show that the police routinely pursue eight different courses of action[5]. Most commonly, they simply leave after listening, without doing anything at all (24 per cent). Next, they give friendly advice about how to avoid a repetition of the incident (16 per cent). Arrest is the next most commonly used action, occurring in 14 per cent of incidents. British police also make arrests in domestic disputes about 23 per cent of the time, they only 'advise' 50 per cent of the time.[6] Police also pointedly warn people what will happen if they are called back; promise future help if it is needed; give explicit advice to one or the other about what they should do to extricate themselves from the conflict; make sure one party leaves the scene; or suggest referral to third parties, professional or otherwise.[7]

The infrequency of arrests is not just true of police responses to disputes. In general, patrol officers, who are responsible for most contacts with the general population, rarely make arrests. In the United States in 1990, police officers made an average of 19 arrests a year.[8] That is less than one arrest per officer every 15 working days. In Canada, police officers make one criminal arrest a month and encounter a recordable criminal offence only once a week.[9]

Although police rarely enforce the law in their manifold encounters with the public, it would be wrong to suggest that the power to arrest is not important. The threat is potent, whatever the outcome of particular encounters. The power to arrest is what makes their intervention authoritative. Police *can* forcibly stop people from doing what they are doing; they *can* push people into bare cells with wet concrete floors and slam shut the heavy barred door behind them. As US police officers sometimes say 'Maybe I can't give 'em a rap (a conviction), but I sure can give them the ride'.

Disputes are not the only situations in which the police are called upon to intervene authoritatively. People come to the police with all sorts of urgent problems hoping they are able to help. These requests, which vastly outnumber disturbances, are as varied as the needs of the public. Such calls require service, not force or law enforcement. In the United States requests of this kind are referred to as 'cats-in-a-tree' situations and in Australia as 'frogs-in-the-drain' cases.

Most patrol work is boring, whether it involves restoring order or providing services. Most of the incidents to which patrol officers respond are routine and undramatic. Los Angeles police estimate that not more than 7 per cent of their dispatched calls require an emergency response. Police in Edmonton, Canada, say 18 per cent, in Seattle 13 per cent, and in Kent, England, 4 per cent. Actually, officers soon learn that often what seems like an emergency probably isn't, so they often dawdle in situations that would seem to require a fast response. Patrol officers spend a lot of time simply waiting for something to happen. They spend most of the time driving methodically around, guided by their extensive knowledge of where incidents are likely to occur. Like tour guides in the museum of human frailty, they can point to houses where they are repeatedly called to mediate family disputes, up-market apartment complexes where young swingers frequently hold noisy parties, troublesome 'biker' bars where drugs are sold, business premises patrolled by a vicious dog, street corners where drug dealers collect, car parks often hit by thieves, warehouses with poor alarm systems and places where police officers have been shot and wounded.

By and large, the people police deal with are life's refugees. Uneducated, poor, often unemployed, they are both victims and victimisers. Hapless, befuddled, beaten by circumstances, people like these turn to the police for the help they can't give themselves. There is little the police can do for them except listen, shrug and move on. The police try to distinguish the few who are genuinely vicious from the majority who are not and treat them differently.

Although patrol work is mostly trivial and non-criminal, it is nonetheless fraught with uncertainty. Officers can never forget that at any moment the boredom of a long shift can be shattered by a call that can be harrowing, traumatic, dangerous or life-threatening. The dilemma for patrol officers is that they must prepare for war even though they are rarely called upon to fight. To relax invites risk; to be constantly on guard invites over-reaction.

Criminal investigation

The next biggest job in policing after patrolling is criminal investigation. It accounts for 14 per cent of police personnel in Canada, 15 per cent in England and Wales and the United States, 16 per cent in Australia and 20 per cent in Japan. Criminal investigation is done by detectives, who do not usually work in uniform and have more flexible hours than patrol officers. Detectives in small police departments or those assigned to field stations tend to be generalists, investigating whatever crime occurs. The rest, usually working out of headquarters, are assigned to speciality units, such as homicide, robbery, vice, narcotics, auto theft and burglary. In recent years some forces have added new specialities such as bias crime, child abuse, sexual assault and computer crime. Like patrol, criminal investigation is overwhelmingly reactive. Whatever preventive effect detectives have comes primarily through deterrence – that is, by removing particular offenders from the streets or by demonstrating to would-be offenders that crime does not pay. Detectives rarely anticipate crime and prevent it from happening. They occasionally 'stake-out' the sites of likely criminal activity or clandestinely watch known criminals in order to catch them in the act. Both tactics have been shown to be costly relative to the amount of criminal activity discovered. Undercover penetration of criminal conspiracies, featured so often in films and television, is rare. A common tactic, especially during the 1980s, was for detectives to pose as people willing to do something illegal, such as buying drugs or receiving stolen property.[10]

What do the vast majority of detectives who investigate crime do? Basically, they talk to people – victims, suspects, witnesses – in order to find out exactly what happened in particular situations and whether there is enough evidence to arrest and prosecute suspects with a reasonable likelihood of conviction. In most cases detectives make very quick judgements about whether an investigation should be undertaken. It depends on two factors: first, whether a credible perpetrator has been fairly clearly identified and, second, whether the crime is especially serious or repugnant – the sort that attracts public attention. Except when forced to do so by public pressure, police do not invest resources in cases in which they have no idea who the criminal might be. Such cases are almost always burglaries and most robberies.

Detectives quickly formulate a theory about who committed the crime and then set about collecting the evidence that will support arrest and prosecution. They know if perpetrators cannot be identified by people on the scene the police are not likely to find the criminals on their own. Nor is physical evidence especially important in determining whether a case is pursued, it is used as confirmation - to support testimony that identifies suspects. The absence of physical evidence might mean a case cannot be made; it may also disconfirm a theory. But it hardly ever leads to the identification of persons not already suspected by the police. In short, criminal investigators begin with the identification, then collect evidence; they rarely collect evidence and then make an identification.

Like doctors in a war zone, criminal investigators employ a triage strategy. If a crime cannot be solved more or less on the spot, the case will probably be closed and the detectives will move on to more promising cases.

Because most crime suspects cannot be identified readily, most crimes go unsolved. Japan is the exception among developed democratic countries. There the police solve about 58 per cent of all crime reported to them. The United States has one of the worst records: only 22 per cent of even the most serious crimes are solved; in England and Wales 35 per cent, in Canada 45 per cent and in Australia 30 per cent. The likelihood of solving a crime varies with the nature of the offence, with higher rates for confrontational crimes and lower rates for property crimes. In the United States police solve 46 per cent of violent crimes against people and 18 per cent of property crimes. Amongst serious crimes, homicide is the most likely to be solved, 67 per cent, and motor vehicle theft the least likely, 15 per cent.[11]

Detectives spend most of their time talking to people strongly suspected of being involved in crimes in an attempt to get them to confess. Interrogations are generally fairly low key and straightforward. Detectives simply confront a suspect with the evidence they have. They do not have to be very clever because most of the time suspects do confess. Sometimes they make threats which have much more to do with the ability of the police to persist than with physical force. Sometimes they bluff and sometimes they cajole.

Detectives also work hard to get 'secondary clearances', that is, when a person who is prosecuted – or sometimes convicted – for one crime confesses to other crimes. Many burglaries are cleared-up in this way. Studies in Britain and the United States indicate that the only sure way for a police force to increase a low clear-up rate is to give more attention to obtaining secondary clearances.[12]

Perhaps the most demanding part of a detective's job is developing expertise in the legal requirements for collecting and reporting evidence. Few have formal legal training, yet they need to understand how prosecutors will use their evidence and the challenges it will face in court. Detectives complain that paperwork is becoming increasingly more intricate and burdensome as a result of changes in court rulings and legislation. Research shows that for every hour detectives talk to people and search for evidence they spend half an hour on paperwork.

Although criminal investigation is regarded as the epitome of policing, it is not at all clear that it requires skills that are peculiar to the police. Many detectives admit off the record that investigation can be done by anyone who is intelligent, poised and willing to learn the intricacies of the criminal law. As one experienced detective chief inspector in England said, 'criminal investigation work is the sort of work any good Prudential insurance man could do'.[13]

Traffic

The third big job the police undertake is the regulation of motor vehicle traffic. In Japan 17 per cent of police officers are assigned to traffic units, 10 per cent in Australia, 7 per cent in England and Wales and the United States and 6 per cent in Canada. Traffic regulation is important for two reasons; first, the number of people killed or injured in traffic accidents and the monetary value of damage to property are substantially higher than result from crime; second, a larger cross section of the populace come into contact with the police through the enforcement of traffic laws than in any other way.

Traffic officers generally work in marked cars patrolling major roads for the purpose of preventing motor vehicle accidents. They do this by enforcing laws against dangerous driving as well as against defective vehicles and by controlling traffic flow in potentially hazardous circumstances, such as those associated with accidents, spillage of toxic substances, parades, sporting events and construction sites. Their work is more self-initiated than that of patrol officers or detectives. They go where the problems are.

Traffic officers tend to be zealous, convinced that what they are doing is very important. They also feel beleaguered, unappreciated and understaffed. Their reaction may have to do with the view among police officers that traffic regulation is peripheral to 'crime fighting'.

Enforcement of traffic laws is a means to an end – maintaining order and safety – not an end in itself. Traffic officers, like patrol officers, use the law as a tool for obtaining compliance. Traffic policing is highly discretionary, requiring officers to make a lot of decisions on the spot whether the law should be enforced. Traffic officers can almost always find an excuse to stop a vehicle, if not for speeding or driving mistakes then for mechanical vehicle defects.

When traffic officers stop a car for a driving violation, their options are not simply whether or not to impose a punishment. They can either apply an official penalty with or without a stern lecture, warn the driver, arrest the driver for being intoxicated or for another crime, or take no action. In England and Wales an official penalty is applied in only 25 per cent of traffic stops.[14]

Other work

Patrol, criminal investigation and traffic regulation are the largest areas of modern operational policing occupying about 85 per cent of all police personnel. Most of the rest is accounted for by administration: 11 per cent in Japan, 10 per cent in Canada, 9 per cent in the United States, 7 per cent in England and Wales and 6 per cent in Australia. Administration includes recruitment, training, public relations and all the housekeeping functions of purchasing, paying, supervising and so forth.

All the other operational units are very small, designed to support patrol, criminal investigation and traffic regulation in specialised ways. The most well known special units are probably the dog squad and the special weapons and tactics team (or SWAT) – these units are used in incidents such as hostage takings or barricaded suspects or rescue operations.

Large police forces may also have permanent formations of riot police – the *Kidotai* in Japan, the Mobile Reserves in England and Wales and the Task Force in New York City. Police forces in cities that are political centres, for example, Tokyo, London and New York are called upon to protect important persons.

The people who must give explicit attention to anticipating and preventing crime, apart from routine uniform patrolling and the under-cover work of a few investigators, barely show up on most organisational charts. Specialised crime prevention units account for 6 per cent of personnel in Japan – by far the largest among the police forces studied. In Australia the figure is 4 per cent, in large United States forces 3 per cent, in Canada 1 per cent, and in England and Wales less than 1 per cent. These 'crime prevention' units are relatively new, dating generally from the 1980s.

Some police forces are also responsible for a number of other activities including inspection and licensing of firearms, bars, liquor stores and gaming parlours; serving of warrants and summons; dealing with lost and found property; background checks on government employees; transporting emergency medical supplies. In short, police often perform a host of ancillary tasks given them by government, largely for reasons of convenience.

The point is that although the police are expected to prevent crime, people expect them to do many other things – things that are not noticed until they are not available.

Variations in police work

Policing is strikingly similar from place to place, at least as indicated by organisational assignments. Among the forces studied about 60 per cent of police personnel patrol and respond to requests for service, 15 per cent investigate crime, 9 per cent regulate traffic and 9 per cent administer. Within countries the proportion of officers assigned to different specialities varies considerably among forces – less in Japan and England and Wales, more in Australia and the United States.

These differences are not systematic, that is, related to features of social context, such as crime rates of population densities. Two factors are indicative. First, the proportions of officers on the major assignments differ very little among urban, suburban and rural police stations. Second, the proportion of officers assigned to different sorts of work has not changed significantly among the forces surveyed during the last 20 years. Among the 18 forces for which historical data were available the proportion of police work in each line of work changed only marginally as shown below.

Average percentage of police officers on different assignments aggregated across countries.

	1970-1975	1986-1990
Patrol	70	59
Criminal investigation	11	15
Traffic	9	8
Administration	7	8
Operational support	13	11
Crime prevention	0	3

Note: Averages have been computed for the two periods because information was not always available for the same beginning and end years from each force. This also explains why the columns total more than 100 per cent.

Although these data do not constitute a definitive test, they suggest that police forces are organised to do the same sorts of work regardless of the social circumstances they confront. Crime and social conditions certainly vary amongst urban, suburban and rural police jurisdictions but police organisations are staffed in almost exactly the same way everywhere. Although social conditions, particularly crime, changed between 1970 and 1990 in the five countries studied, police organisations did not. What the police are prepared to do does not change with what needs doing.

There are several reasons for this. The first is bureaucratic politics. Existing organisational units fight hard to maintain their share of resources. A second reason is that police forces are sometimes compelled to adhere to national standards for staffing. In England and Wales Her Majesty's Inspectorate of Constabulary, a central government agency, monitors force staffing patterns and recommends adjustments to fit the preferred model. In Japan the National Police Agency has the same functions. In the United States so-far voluntary processes of accreditation exert the same homogenizing effect.

Finally, police officers are part of an international professional culture, reinforced by conferences, seminars and workshops, exchanges of personnel and trade publications. They continually look over their shoulders to determine whether their forces follow what the profession considers 'efficient, modern and progressive'. In short, they copy one another, especially a few 'flagship' forces such as Los Angeles and New York City, the London Metropolitan Police and the Royal Canadian Mounted Police.

For all these reasons, police organisations do not adapt to the work they must do. Rather the work they must do is adapted to the police organisation.

References

1. Bayley, D.H. (1985) *Patterns of Policing*. New Brunswick NJ: Rutgers University Press.
2. Whitaker, G. *et al* (1981) *Measuring Police Agency Performance*. Washington DC: Law Enforcement Assistance Agency. Mimeo.
   Morris, P. and Heal, K. (1981) *Crime Control and the Police: A Review of Research*. Home Office Research Study No. 67. London: HMSO.
   Thames Valley Police (1991) *Annual Report of the Chief Constable*.
3. Gilsinian, J.F. (1989) They is clowning tough: 911 and the social construction of reality. *Criminology*, 27, pp 329-344.
   Reiss, A.J. (1971) *The Politics of the Police*. New Haven: Yale University Press.
4. Bittner, E. (1970) *The Functions of the Police in Modern Society: a Review of Background Factors, Current Practices and Possible Role Models*. Chevy Chase, MD: National Institute of Mental Health.

5. Bayley, D.H. (1986) The tactical choice of police patrol officers. *Journal of Criminal Justice*, 14, pp 329-348.

6. Shapland, J. and Hobbs, D. (1989) Policing priorities on the ground. In Morgan, R. and Smith D. H. (eds) *Coming to Terms with Policing*. London: Routledge.

7. McIver, J.P. and Parks, R.B. (1981) Evaluating police performance. In Bennett, R. (ed) *Police at Work: Policy Issues and Analysis*. Beverly Hills CA: Sage Publications.

8. Bureau of Justice Statistics (1988, 1990, 1991) *Sourcebook of Criminal Justice Statistics*. Washington DC: Government Printing Office.

9. Ericson, R.V. and Shearing, C.D. (1986) The scientification of police work. In Bohme, G. and Stehr, N. (eds) *The Knowledge Society*. Dordrecht: D. Reidel Publishing Company.

10. Marx, G.T. (1988) *Undercover Police Work: the Paradoxes and Problems of a Necessary Evil*. Berkeley: University of California Press.

11. Bureau of Justice Statistics (1988, 1990, 1991) *Sourcebook of Criminal Justice Statistics*. Washington DC: Government Printing Office.

12. Eck, J.E. (1982) *Problem Solving: the Investigation of Residential Burglary and Robbery*. Washington DC: Police Executive Research Forum.
Burrows, J. (1986) *Investigating Burglary: the Measurement of Police Performance*. Home Office Research Study No. 88. London: HMSO.

13. McClure, J. (1980) *Spike Island: Portrait of a British Police Division*. New York: Pantheon Books.

14. Skogan, W.C. (1990) *Police and the Public in England and Wales: a British Crime Survey Report*. Home Office Research Study No. 117. London: HMSO.

Enforcement, Service and Community Models of Policing

Nigel Fielding

Summary

- The enforcement model of policing concentrates on the control of crime and the enforcement of the law. It enjoys clarity of purpose and it requires little from the public other than consent and tax revenue. Its hierarchial organisation does not well suit other demands on the police and it is not especially successful in addressing the goals which it sets itself.

- In the service model, policing priorities are set in consultation with the public. It requires an organisational structure that permits planning to take account of frequent changes in priorities, and would constantly have to re-think the balance of effort expended on crime control, order maintenance and general services.

- The community model gives precedence to maintaining order and public tranquillity over crime control, with the police and the community sharing responsibility for dealing with crime and disorder. It emphasises the role of patrol officers, who have long-term assignments to particular beats, and partnerships with local social agencies. The organisational structure has to accommodate the demands of teamworking.

- There is no perfect model of policing and it is probably necessary to borrow elements from each model to arrive at a police service that meets all the demands of the public.

Introduction

Academic studies of the police have tended to concentrate on empirical studies of their functions and discursive analyses of the culture of policing but relatively little attention has been paid to the theory of policing. In what follows an attempt will be made to characterise three broad models of policing: the enforcement model, the service model, and the community (or geographic responsibility) model. Each will be examined by reference to its philosophy, organisational structure, management policy, and operational strategy and tactics. In a final section, comment is made on the evaluation of these models.

Our research knowledge of the different models varies. As the established approach most is known about the enforcement model while least is known about the community model. The models are analytic constructions and one would not expect to encounter policing systems in the real world that were pure examples of any single model.

The enforcement model

Philosophy

An organisation's mandate is what society expects of it. The mandate exercises compelling influence on organisation members; they take it to heart in their understanding of what they should do, the priorities they should pursue and the ways they should validate their work. The police mandate is commonly understood to be law enforcement. It can be argued that this is a misconception. Sir Robert Peel, in founding the 'new police', was clear that order maintenance was the precedent condition for the exercise of law enforcement and that the community's consent and support was needed before enforcement could effectively proceed. But this emphasis is now more familiar to constitutional lawyers than to the police, and what matters most in understanding everyday police work is that the lower ranks believe that their mission is law enforcement. This leads to preoccupation with the speed of response; with deterrence in terms of a uniformed presence on the streets; and arrests, with effectiveness perceived in terms of detection and clear-up rates. This prompts a crisis reactive policing style depending on citizens to invoke the 'fire brigade' response.

In the enforcement approach the police gain their authority from the law which defines and limits their role. The police apply the law in the statute books, as interpreted by the courts. Work beyond the brief provided by the law is the province of other agencies. The notion offers clarity of purpose. It brings consistency to police work and a clear focus for training. By and large, the authority of the police under the enforcement model is that which we recognise from police histories:

43

firm, fair and blinkered. 'Fair' means that police take their place as dispassionate evidence-gatherers feeding an adversarial justice system. The police service is a powerful institution, granted effective monopoly of the use of physical force in civil society. This power is controlled by two doctrines which must be finely balanced. The first is that the police are the exclusive repository of law enforcement action. The community has a passive role, volunteering information when required to, bearing witness, paying the police levy through taxes. The community is to support the police and to grant them autonomy over their field of professional expertise, provided it is narrowly defined as the enforcement of law without fear or favour.

The second balancing doctrine is that the police are, and must be, apolitical. Officers may not hold political office, are denied membership of 'normal' employees' organisations, and must be chary of involvement in community organisations. At an institutional level, the tripartite system offers a constrained accountability designed to keep both community and central government at arms length from 'operational' policing decisions. The Nuremberg defence is not only available but sacred: the police follow the orders codified in law. If one wishes to change policing one must change the law.

Organisational structure

The law enforcement model tends towards a quasi-military form of bureaucratic organisation, the pyramid shape of the classic organisation chart, which is formalised, rule-oriented and standardised. The Sheehy Inquiry[1] criticised the negative motivational, productivity and ethical consequences of such hierarchies.

It is paradoxical that the ranks lowest in the hierarchy enjoy the greatest discretion. The patrol officers are the interface of organisation and public. Supervision is distant and patchy. Decisions are personal and largely non-reviewable, since each constable controls the means by which superiors hear of their actions. The chief officer's discretion is constrained by relations with the Home Office and the police authority. A powerful Discipline Code applies to subordinates whose occupational deviance happens to become visible to supervisors. There is centralisation of management, with all roads leading to force headquarters. At station level the pyramid is replicated. The law enforcement approach offers a finely-tuned reactive machine with a limited capacity for proactive intervention.

Output

The organisation is most comfortable in delivering fast response to public demands for action but criminal investigation and crime prevention must also be addressed. Since an effective response to such demands cannot be provided by reactive patrol units, such functions are undertaken by specialists. But the hierarchical organisation inhibits communication across ranks and functions and obstructs the pooling of information, teamwork and planning. Because information is a valuable resource enabling personal advancement, individuals in specialist units and in routine patrol sections may reserve it to themselves. Problems of poor working relations interfere with crime investigation.

The reactive posture leads the police to prioritise short-term information with a direct payoff. Community constables may hold local knowledge offering a good basis for crime pattern analysis, but making such information available to managers who could form an overview falls foul of divisions of rank and status. There are worries about other units 'pinching' a case upon which one has expended effort. Detectives look down on uniformed officers and may disparage information from them. Uniformed officers resent the status of detectives and will not pass on what they know.

While crime collators draw information together, the reactive posture makes for haphazard use of it. Collated crime information is not kept in a form enabling crime pattern analysis. Ideally, local crime statistics would support a strategy in which crime patterns were identified and deployment of officers attuned to it. Instead, assignment is often done by working through an established list of functions with little accommodation to the geographical or temporal distribution of demand.

The notoriously separate world of the CID is an obstacle to teamwork. It is a closed elite and somewhat divorced from public priorities. Determining the balance of effort between the investigation, say, of burglary relative to racial attacks, is done on criteria unresponsive to public concerns and fears. Links between detectives and community groups like Neighbourhood Watches are even more remote than those between detectives and other police units.

Crime prevention poses a challenge to a reactive law enforcement organisation. The more time is spent spreading the crime prevention message to businesses, local authorities and homeowners the more distant those officers responsible become from the core units of the organisation. It is believed that uniformed patrol has a crime prevention role, providing a deterrent effect by 'showing the flag'. Comparing crime rates in similar areas with low and high levels of uniformed patrol suggests the effect is limited.

Management policy

The law enforcement model bespeaks a closed organisation, resistant to influence from the community, and operating to an internally-defined agenda. Communication and management is top down and command-oriented. This means that orders must be issued before things happen, thus delaying response. Managers are liable to be led by subordinates because they control information about the interface with the public.

Authority is distributed by rank. Much effort is expended in job demarcation. The trappings of office necessary to make each rank distinctive divide the organisation. As people move up the hierarchy the skills they have developed may be lost if the skills are tied to the functional responsibility of a particular rank. Promotion is by longevity as well as merit. Personnel control is rule-oriented and punishment-centred.

Leadership resides in the office. Incumbents may interpret their role flexibly but decisions are reviewable only by those of higher rank. At the most senior levels this may lead to quirky variations in policy which reflect the orientation of a particular officer. At intermediate and lower levels incumbents adopt a reactive posture as little is to be gained by initiative or anticipation.

Management prefers quantitative measures of productivity and effectiveness, such as arrest and process figures. While readily counted, these may not give a good reflection of the quality of service and do not take account of performance criteria which much affect the public's regard for what the police do.

Operational strategies and tactics

Police organisations which are primarily oriented to crime control have the great advantage of providing what is widely perceived by the public and most police officers as the *raison d'être* of the police institution. But 'law and order' encompasses order maintenance as well as law enforcement. The maintenance of public order represents a trying test for the police. Several of the most notorious cases which have prompted disenchantment with contemporary policing, and allegations of corruption, bias and incompetence have related to public order. Too great an emphasis on enforcement risks disturbing the relationship between the police and the public.

In the law enforcement model organisational routines and procedures are set by the crime control orientation. The functional units, the proportion of personnel in each unit, their training and competencies, procedures and relations with other agencies are based on the process for criminal cases. The police 'wait' for a crime to occur and then proceed with well-rehearsed routines. Such routines are more appropriate for some kinds of demand for services than others.

In a literal sense the organisation which adopts a reactive stance is 'controlled' by the public, for it is the public which activates demand for service. The organisation waits for a crime to be notified by someone. There is no need to diagnose the nature of crime in general. The organisation works with what it is given by the public. Crime is incident-specific. Repeated incidents of a similar *modus operandi* will prompt efforts to detect a pattern, but the organisation is not set up to consider more broadly the shifts in patterns of crime across a jurisdiction. In this respect it is difficult to think in terms of operational strategies.

Thus, it is no surprise that in recent years the police have been caught out by unanticipated public sensitivity in at least two areas: crimes against women, particularly the handling of rape investigations and domestic violence, and racially-motivated assaults. There are a number of notorious instances where the traditional approach failed, with negative effects on police/public relations and to the cost of many victims whose suffering was aggravated by secondary victimisation inflicted by the system. The law enforcement model makes poor provision for victims' needs.

Looking at routine patrol, the response to calls for service involves rapid response or 'fire brigade policing'. It is mobile-based, leading to the recent issuing by the Home Office of precise time limits for response to various types of call, regardless of the characteristics of the area policed, the resources available or the nature of demand. The stopwatch approach to performance measurement is consistent with the use of quantitative performance measures. It is precise, readily-monitored from above, easily-tabulated for external consumption but provides only a limited index of quality of service.

The reactive rapid response tactic is indiscriminate. Studies of the information provided to patrols by despatchers indicate that it is often so scanty that it is difficult for officers to anticipate what will meet them on arrival at the scene. A high proportion of calls from the public are trivial but without screening it is hard to judge which will prove to be serious, so it seems safest always to offer a full patrol response. Response at the scene of the incident is characterised by 'load shedding'. Patrol officers have to be ready to respond at any moment to the next demand. Their preoccupation is first to determine what exactly is happening, second to determine if an arrestable offence has been committed and, if not, to clear the scene as rapidly as possible. The 'load' may later be shed by referral on to another agency although there is no monitoring of outcomes.

Patrolling is organised on a shift system which is only loosely calibrated with the incidence of demand. Demands for police service vary in volume and type over the twenty-four hour cycle, but the numbers available depend on the personnel establishment and the numbers 'abstracted' for training, sick leave and so on. Some urban stations can regularly muster only half the officers nominally required to staff a shift.

Despite efforts at 'directed patrol', where officers are assigned to deal with a particular problem on a given shift, patrol is largely random. Directed patrol relies on sufficient officers being available. Since this condition seldom obtains, patrol is generally 'unassigned' waiting for a call. The nature of response rests not with supervisors but with constables. They take the calls and they respond to them. Supervision and direction are largely passive.

Criminal investigation is a specialist function with little patrol involvement in the investigation of cases. The detective effort is centralised and not only aloof from other police functions but from the broader public.

The service model

Philosophy

In this country the best example of a service model of policing is represented by rural constabularies.[2] Where volumes of crime were low, and the resources available to the constabulary were limited by a restricted tax base, the service model grew up. While this model accommodates crime control, its daily routine is dominated by service-type relations with the public. Major crime is a rare occurrence and may require assistance from metropolitan forces more experienced in its investigation. If there is a major incident of public disorder help will be sought from other sources (historically, the militia and special constabulary).

Organisational structure

There is little to distinguish the organisation of the traditional service model from the law enforcement model. The bureaucratic foci of the organisation remain the constabulary headquarters and the divisional/station hierarchy. The rhythm of local stations is seldom disturbed but, when it is, the line of authority more quickly leads to headquarters. The headquarters is highly responsive to what were once called 'landed interests' and it is a major purchaser of goods and services from local businesses.

Specialisation is affected both by the constraint on resources and the restricted opportunities for circulation of officers between different roles. Specialist functions involve small numbers of officers who stay longer in the job. There is, no doubt, a balance to be sought between the growth of expertise and burn-out as a result of having done the same thing for many years.

Output

The service model features a close responsiveness to what the community wants and is largely reactive. Priorities are set by consultation with the public largely through social occasions and a host of informal contacts with established local interests such as landowners and the business community.

In the abstract, public concerns could be built into the priority-setting process of the service model via some type of community forum. There could be meetings whose membership reflected an effort to identify all those with an interest in the provision of police services. Initially, meetings would not involve the police doing more than recording demands and then examining how such demands might be met, taking account of conflicts between different demands and the resources available. There would be further meetings at which police thinking was explained, community interests would be able to lobby for their demands, followed by negotiation, and finally resulting in the publication of an annual plan for policing priorities.

Management policy

If there were a force which took so seriously the public role in priority-setting, it would require not only an organisational structure set up to permit planning and to change those plans on short timescales, but a managerial style quite different from that practised by the traditional police hierarchies. This is because, once priorities had been set, the organisation would have to respond to the lobbying it had stimulated. Each officer in contact with the public would have distinctive local interests to represent which might lead them into direct contact with superior officers. This would have to be accepted as a basis for a greater measure of independence so long as responsiveness to local interests remained the priority.[3]

There would be a need for liaison officers at the divisional/area level, and at the station level, to spend time on running and maintaining the consultative process. The liaison role would have to be created by robbing operational roles.

Since this force would be more open to the public it would expect the public to provide it with assistance. For instance, there should be no need to orchestrate Neighbourhood Watch schemes, because the higher level of public contact with the force would result in routine reporting of suspicious circumstances.

Operational strategy and tactics

Assuming no change in resources, a service-oriented force would have to re-think the balance of effort it expended on crime control, order maintenance and general services. If, for instance, the community got police to accept that they should expend effort in teaching schoolchildren the rudiments of lawful conduct and 'citizenship', this would deplete the number of officers available for general patrol.

Experience with public consultation, even in some urban areas, suggests that the concerns of local people are seldom about serious crimes, they are most likely to be about car crime and residential burglary. But even these offences are not regular events in most areas. The police would have to expect to deal with complaints about parking, noisy neighbours and loose dogs, matters dealt with by other agencies under the enforcement model.

The service model takes the police a long way from their usual priorities. They, especially outside cities, are not unused to requests for services. But they are usually able to turn the problem over to another agency. They are also used to dealing with complaints about behaviour that is a nuisance rather than a crime by soothing the complainants. Under the service model they would have to take some action.

The service model could not adhere to existing quantitative performance measures. The shift in priorities would soon indicate a significant decline in traditional indicators of arrest and process and there would be large fluctuations from one year to the next, as priorities were changed. With some responsibilities new qualitative indicators would have to be adopted. For example, if priority were given to educating schoolchildren in citizenship, an indicator would be required of how effective the lessons had been.

In the service model the insulation of detectives from the public could be broken down by involving them in the priority-setting public meetings. The model requires explaining why service cannot be provided or why things have gone wrong when there is a complaint. These are pressures from which the enforcement model is free.

The community model

Philosophy

The enforcement and service models of policing are at opposite ends of the spectrum with the community model mixing elements of both. Authoritative sources have expressed a commitment to sector policing, which is a system of geographic responsibility policing with considerable affinity to the community model. Yet considerable doubts remain, not least because research on community policing as it has been practised in Britain is pessimistic about its effectiveness. My research on community policing in police divisions with favourable conditions suggested it has a potential which has not been realised.[4] Because a systematic experiment integrating all the key elements of the approach is still awaited it is necessary to speculate on what might be rather than to refer to what 'is'.

Compared with the enforcement model, the community policing approach takes a different inspiration from the police mandate. Civil order, peace and security are given priority over crime control, which is seen as a means of enhancing peace and security. This approach accords with the idea that the first and pre-eminent duty of the police is to secure public tranquillity.[5] In this conception of their mandate, the police derive their authority from society or, in common law terms, from the community as it grants that authority through law. In the community model the police are an agency of local government and the community. The role of central government would be less. The police role would be socially-defined. The question is, in what areas and to what degree?

It is necessary to differentiate between community policing as the more responsive provision of conventional police services, and the pursuit of 'outreach' functions. This is an established tension in community policing. For example, should community policing entail promoting 'community spirit' or should it involve making the provision of traditional police services more accessible by, for instance, setting up police offices on high-crime estates?

The core of the community policing model is generally agreed to be the provision of patrol constables who have long-term assignments to a particular beat. To this may be added the institution of public consultation mechanisms with a brief to focus on problems of crime and order. These are the principal elements of the sector policing approach now being advocated by bodies such as the Inspectorate of Constabulary, the Association of Chief Police Officers, and the Audit Commission.

The model is not preoccupied with 'outreach' but with public order and law enforcement. It is, however, committed to delivering those traditional ends by new means. Neither public order nor crime are seen as problems exclusively to be handled by the police. New relationships are created with agencies now seen as partners (including agencies with whom police have had a poor relationship). Local authorities (especially housing departments), architects, businesses, social services, voluntary agencies, the probation service, the courts and prosecution service are among the other agencies with a role. This broad brief demands much effort in servicing inter-agency relationships. It requires officers to adopt a more forthcoming posture than may be usual. Because they represent the organisation, they *are* the police for the purpose of meeting other agencies. The model requires officers to be granted more autonomy and responsibility than the hierarchical approach willingly grants.

Crime control is not discarded but its diagnosis is broadened; officers have to seek ways of responding to social problems that have criminogenic influence but which may carry them a long way from the services they have customarily provided. A good contemporary example is that of drug law enforcement. Police in liaison with 'street' drug agencies are obliged to turn a blind eye to offending, such as the unauthorised possession of drugs, as partners in a joint effort which, among other things, provides clean drug-taking equipment to reduce the risk of AIDS.

The model also offers the community a more active role. The means by which this is done are similar to the consultative mechanisms described for the service model, but the agenda is focused on crime and order. Rather than local people having a major say in setting priorities but leaving it to police to prosecute them, the public also has a role in the control of crime and the maintenance of order. The mechanisms are familiar as Neighbourhood Watch and Business Watch schemes, and the 'parish constable' has latterly joined the long tradition of the special constabulary. The community is also a client of policing services. Thus, there is a role for opinion surveys and other means of determining levels of satisfaction with policing.

The difficulties that the police face in pursuing a community-based response to crime and public disorder arise from the nature of contemporary social bonds, particularly in urban areas. There has been a change from 'community' to 'association', where bonds are not geo-local but revolve around particular interests shared with a network of people who may be widely separated in terms of space and who may have little in common except for the particular interest which brings them into association from time to time.[6] This weakens the tie of purely local bonds. There is also a class effect. The pursuit of non-geo-local bonds is for the socially mobile and the relatively well-off. Those still relying on the local community for their social network are the poor, the disabled and the elderly.

This suggests that the pursuit by the police of 'community spirit' may be a forlorn enterprise. There is doubt whether any agency can achieve it, and the police are among the least likely to do so. This is another reason for focusing scrupulously on those parts of the police mandate with which local people are most likely to identify, namely, the direct control of crime. Neighbourhood Watch, which benefits from a degree of self-interest, can contribute, but the core effort remains with the police and their provision of a high level of foot patrol. Much has been made of the public role by advocates of the community approach, but the greater contribution is likely to be made by partner agencies than by the public. The main role of the public is as client and as consultee in the priority-setting process.

In the enforcement model the police maintain a posture of being apolitical. In the community model the police acknowledge a 'political' role, not in the sense of party politics but in mediating interests. They are long used to mediating the conflict of parties to industrial conflict, racial conflict, religious conflict and indeed social conflict of all sorts.[7] By their handling of public events, their responsiveness to sectional community interests, party politics, local authority police committees, and the Home Office, the police play a role that is inescapably and fundamentally political. It is likely that the more explicitly political role required by the community model will excite controversy from time to time.

The model supposes that police are engaged in a relationship of mutual responsibility with community and political representatives. But any thoughtful approach to 'the community' sees there is not one community but many. While the police are to be responsive to priorities and demands as represented to them, these various groups are responsive to operational practicalities upon which the police are the experts. This means that police will be in the position of explaining what must be neglected if some particular interest is emphasised. Implicitly this means the police abandoning an exclusive say over 'operational matters'. If operational matters are open to discussion and debate, the same must apply to broader matters of policy.

Organisational structure

The organisational structure under a community policing model will have to differ from that of an enforcement model. In particular, 'rules' would have to be adapted to fit the situation, since service delivery would vary by the nature of the community policed, agreed priorities and so on. Further, since officers' responsibilities would be more externally-directed by taking account of community expectations, they would be less closely bound by the rank structure and more by their effectiveness as seen by external audiences. This would subtly undermine the structuring of working relationships based solely on rank. The result could be a more collegial atmosphere, where divisions of rank were weaker and where a series of temporary working relationships to respond to various demands would expose officers to a greater range of intra-organisational contacts. But this could also make for uncertainty and occupational deviance; new criteria for the exercise of discretion would be required, with changes to training and staff appraisal. The challenge to the organisational environment and culture of the police posed by the community model should not be underestimated.

Devolution of authority and management function is a central element in the declared commitment to sector policing. Local police commanders will need more autonomy, including budgetary control. It follows that, in order to protect the interests of taxpayers, they would also have to bear greater responsibility if things go wrong in terms of, say, excessive overtime payments in response to some particular local problem.

The community model presses for adoption of a flatter rank structure, with fewer managerial grades and more frontline grades. There would be less functional specialisation because frontline officers – patrol constables and sergeants – would be expected to cope with a range of new demands. It rewards constables who become generalists, drawing on skills and tactics relevant not only to crime control but to negotiation of demand, consultation and information-gathering.

Management policy

Internal communication would involve 'downwards' consultation. Mechanisms would be needed by which feedback from frontline officers could be garnered and then evaluated. As information flowed up the organisation for decision, interim statements of likely decisions would need to be offered back for assessment by frontline officers. A monitoring function would be necessary in respect of schemes and programmes, akin to the role of 'research and information officers' in the Probation Service. This approach to communication would also work against formality and rank-based deference.

Managerial authority would not come from rank but from knowledge and contribution; it is already the case that in some specialist functions lower rank officers enjoy a better grasp of the job than those who manage them. A good example is child protection, where junior (often female) detectives gain a sophisticated grasp of special interviewing techniques needed to assess child witness evidence. Supervisory officers may find that they cannot assess their juniors' work because they do not have a working knowledge of it, so changes to training and appraisal would be necessary. Promotion would be performance-based, with an assessment of the officer's value to the organisation.

Personnel control would also have to shift, from being punishment-centred (as in the enforcement model) to being reward-oriented. A flatter hierarchy and assignment by expertise not by rank calls for new means of creating incentives and rewarding achievement. These elements of the model are closely akin to developments in industry, from which notions of total quality management, quality circles and so on have been derived. One of the major benefits of this approach is enhanced job satisfaction so that management and supervision become less significant as a means of regulating conduct.

Leadership is participatory rather than by rank. More responsibility is delegated but there is better front-line knowledge to assess whether individuals are measuring up to their responsibilities. Managers can be more proactive because they have more contact with lower ranks, rather than relying on annual appraisal or the promotion process.

A broader range of information would have to be available to managers so that they could assess performance. As well as things that can be quantified, like the number of arrests, there would be a need to draw on, for example, assessments of the quality of interventions in public consultation meetings, and whether officers had solved problems they had explicitly set out to tackle.

Operational strategy and tactics

Although the community model emphasises a problem-solving approach the need for reactive, fast response service delivery remains. Call screening and call analysis become imperative to differentiate the response to calls for service. The response to a call may be referral to some other agency. Unlike the 'load shedding' of the enforcement model the community model approach is 'load sharing'. To ensure that 'sharing' did not become 'shedding', liaison roles would have to be created.

The caseload of detectives would be reduced by case screening to filter cases purely for them and those which could be handled by patrol constables. Giving patrol constables more ownership of cases that came up on their beats would promote sharing of information. There would be a need for the training of patrol constables to be extended.

Some versions of the model suggest decentralisation of some CID services to support patrol teams. There is already experience with the devolution of burglary investigation to uniformed patrols. If more units are involved in investigation then there may be more analysis of crime problems; frontline officers may be able to identify reasons behind fluctuations in crime rates. But there would be a danger that if many individuals were involved in investigating a particular crime the effort could become diffused.

The community model, as described here, emphasises patrol and a territorial basis of responsibility. The system is based on beats, where constables gain a sense of beat 'ownership' and responsibility. Urban beats may be local but they represent large numbers of residents, more than one constable could hope to know. Thus, the community model requires a team perspective, drawing on the functional links and multi-agency partnerships. Where there is teamwork there is an incentive to plan interventions, pursuing a proactive, problem-oriented brief.

The main way in which crime prevention becomes a basic patrol strategy is by the regular, predictable availability of a known officer to whom information can be given. Long-term beat assignment is seen as encouraging the growth of trust when residents know the information they pass on will be acted on in a way that is sensitive to their interests. To ensure continuity, and to allow for training and temporary cover, the police establishment might need to be increased. A new relationship would be required between beat constable sections and the smaller number of reactive patrols needed to cope with emergencies and unpredictable demands.

More widespread adoption of the community model would have to secure public and organisational commitment. The associated costs would only be warranted if improvements were seen in order maintenance and crime control. They would not be warranted simply by improvement in general ratings of the police/public relationship.

Evaluating models of policing

There is no perfect model of policing, nor is there any policing system which is a perfect instance of a single model. Nevertheless, some broad assessment can be made of the difficulties arising from an over-emphasis on each ideal-typical model. The enforcement model offers a forceful reactive machine which proceeds by its own dictates once activated by the public. Its emphasis on crime control leads to the neglect of other demands and interests. It is primarily a crisis response model. It favours a quasi-military organisation with strong centralizing tendencies, making co-operation and communication across the organisation difficult. Demands calling on particular skills are handled by the creation of specialisms. It measures its success quantitatively. Its demerits are the reason so many people are spending so much time looking at alternative ways of delivering police service.

The service model is even more reactive to public demands than the enforcement model. The involvement of the public extends to re-thinking the balance between crime control and the provision of social services. This would lead to a more open organisation but one in continual crisis about its purposes. It gives the political process a higher profile, with the potential to impose frequent changes of priority. Resources to effect crime control would be squeezed in favour of the provision of community services. Such services may have an impact upon crime and order, but the effect would be diffuse and hard to measure.

The community model is construed as a mixed model. It puts maintaining order before law enforcement. It assumes that order must be achieved to gain the consent and co-operation of the community so that enforcement can proceed efficiently. It seeks to enhance the community's role to maximise the information available for the pursuit and prosecution of those who create crime and disorder, not primarily because it wishes to promote social integration. The problems of the community model lie in the organisational environment, internal relationships, the status of patrol work, and the belief that the public can play a *direct* role in policing.

There are many subtleties in choosing the model, or the elements of the model, which we should favour. There is a need to distinguish between the 'hard' and 'soft' output measures of policing. If the police employ a tough campaign to solve a lot of burglaries and arrest many burglars, this is hard output. The effect may be that the number of burglaries diminishes. People may feel safer and give the police better performance ratings, which is soft output. But the changes may be partly caused by better surveillance or by a campaign for installing better locks on doors. One measure supports the enforcement model, the other the crime prevention element of the community model. It is therefore difficult to know which element of service delivery has produced the desired effect; indeed, both may have done so. We are probably in the business of borrowing elements from each model rather than endorsing one in its entirety. Once we do this we are in the realm of balancing factors, which carries with it the implication that an exaggeration of any single approach will prove counter-productive.

References

1. Home Office (1993) *Inquiry into Police Responsibilities and Rewards* (The Sheehy Report). London: HMSO.
2. Young, M. (1993) *In the Sticks: Cultural Identity in a Rural Police Force*. Oxford: Clarendon.

3. Grimshaw, R. and Jefferson, T. (1987) *Interpreting Police Work.* London: Allen and Unwin.
4. Fielding, N. (1995) *Community Policing.* Oxford: Clarendon.
5. Reiner, R. (1985) *The Politics of the Police.* Brighton: Wheatsheaf.
6. Tonnies, F. (1950) *Community and Association.* London: Routledge and Kegan Paul.
7. Fielding, N. (1991) *The Police and Social Conflict.* London: Athlone.

The Police Patrol Function: What Research Can Tell Us

Michael Hough

Summary

- Patrol work absorbs the majority of police manpower and financial resources.

- Uniformed patrols undertake a variety of functions, many of which are unrelated, or only tangentially related, to crime. Central to this work are concepts of 'emergency' and public order.

- Changes at the margin in patrol presence will probably go unnoticed by the public and would-be offenders and are unlikely to affect crime rates.

- Substantial increases in patrol presence will be noticed, and will prevent opportunistic crimes, while crimes involving planning and preparation are more likely to be displaced over time, place or method.

- Increasing levels of foot patrol can reduce public fear of crime and increase public satisfaction with the police.

- Rapid response to calls for help has few immediate pay-offs in terms of offence clear-up rates. Achieving rapid response is less important than setting up clear expectations about response and then meeting them.

- Community policing strategies which assign officers long-term to geographically defined areas, and those which involve high levels of contact with the public, can increase public ratings of the police and reduce fear of crime.

- Problem-oriented policing has been shown to reduce levels of crime and disorder, and should also yield the benefits associated with community policing in terms of public satisfaction and reduced fear of crime.

Introduction

Only three decades ago the British police service was an institution which was largely closed both to social research and to the somewhat analogous attention of 'current affairs' journalists. Public understanding of the realities of policing was limited, and views in the 1960s were arguably far more polarised than they are today. For many, the police were still set firmly on a pedestal, as the 'best police force in the world', with the 'British bobbie' regarded as the epitome of national character.[1] Towards the end of the 1960s, on the other hand, the counter-culture view of 'the Pigs' as an institution fit only for ridicule had become surprisingly well established not only amongst the young but amongst liberal opinion formers. Social research since then has helped promote a better and more balanced understanding of the police, and a clearer idea both of the competencies of the police and of the limits to these competencies.

Police research in the United States established itself in the 1960s, and several large-scale empirical studies were conducted over the next decade. The British police began to open up to researchers in the 1970s – although compared with the United States the level of investment in research has been small.

The work in the United States has been an important, if questionable, reference point for British researchers. The broad conclusions about the impact of policing strategies on crime can probably be safely imported here although the balance between systems of formal and informal control, and their degree of interdependence, obviously varies substantially between cultures.

This paper summarises what can be said on the basis of properly conducted empirical research about the impact of uniformed police patrol work on crime. It refers to the key pieces of research carried out over the last 25 years which collectively have made a substantial contribution to re-shaping ideas about the police and policing policy. It then considers research on more recent policing strategies such as community and neighbourhood policing, sector policing and problem-oriented policing.

The patrol function

Before the 1970s there had been remarkably little research, at least in this country, on the patrol function. Not surprisingly, when researchers did gain access to the police, much of the research was iconoclastic, in that it corrected misperceptions which were widespread outside of the police service. Researchers' first 'discovery' was that only a minority of patrol work was directly crime-related.[2] In contrast to public perceptions at least, the uniformed police spent little time – somewhere between a fifth and a third, depending largely on counting conventions – actually dealing with crimes; a substantial proportion of their time was spent on non-criminal incidents, and the balance on apparently unfocused and unproductive patrolling.

Curiously in hindsight, much of this early research paid little attention to the – now fairly obvious – connections between the policing of crime and the handling of disorder, though there were important exceptions.[3] The central role of the police in tackling emergencies was also substantially ignored, despite the (now oft-cited) work of Egon Bittner.[4] His analysis of precisely what is unique to the uniformed police function is worth quoting. Incidents become matters for the police, he argued, not by virtue of their illegality but because they were emergencies – 'something which ought not to be happening and about which someone had better do something now'. He argued that the specific competence of the police lies in their capacity for decisive action, which

...derives from the authority to overpower opposition in the 'there-and-then' of the situation of action. The policeman, and the policeman alone, is equipped, entitled and required to deal with every exigency in which force may have to be used to meet it.

A second set of descriptive studies established that the police are heavily dependent on the public for information about crime.[5] In the absence of any information to the contrary, it was generally assumed that the police played a central role in the discovery of those crimes with which they dealt. (This assumption was shared by radical critics of the police, who argued that selective policing shaped the characteristics of offenders reaching official attention.) However, research on both sides of the Atlantic found that of crimes known to the police, little more than a tenth are discovered by the police themselves.[6] In the vast majority of cases, victims or people acting on their behalf report crimes to the police. Further research, in the shape of national and local victim surveys, gave a much clearer idea of the small proportion of crime which reaches police attention. The British Crime Survey, for example, has shown that well under half of crimes against individuals or their private property are reported to the police; less than a third end up in police records[7]; and in only 7 per cent of crimes can the police put a name to the offender.[8]

A final set of descriptive studies mainly carried out in the 1970s[9] all portrayed a remarkably consistent picture of the extensive autonomy of police officers 'on the ground' – whereby police discretion increases as one moves *down* the hierarchy. That police work necessarily involves the exercise of discretion is an idea which is now so well embedded in assumptions about the police that it may seem surprising that, like the non-criminal work of uniformed patrols, police discretion had to be 'discovered' by social scientists. The fact that it did says a great deal about the perceptions – or misperceptions – about policing which had currency at the time: a commonly drawn analogy was a military one, that uniformed patrols were troops ready to be deployed against crime by their commanders as and when requirements dictated. The extent of police discretion came as a surprise only against the background of such assumptions. The existence of discretion was sometimes taken to imply that the workforce would successfully subvert any crime-fighting strategies imposed by managers. With the benefit of hindsight, however, this conclusion seems overstated. There is nothing unique in the extent of police discretion, and police managers share with many others the problems of maintaining managerial control over a dispersed workforce operating in an unpredictable environment.

The impact of patrols on crime

If the results of these pieces of research called into question the conventional views of the day about the police as an organisation which was primarily devoted to crime-fighting, the most influential pieces of iconoclastic research in the 1970s were undoubtedly a series of experimental studies carried out in the United States. The best known of these is the Kansas City Preventive Patrol Experiment.[10] This was, particularly by the standards of the day, an enormously painstaking and expensive analysis of the impact of varying levels of mobile patrol in one part of Kansas City. It showed that a two or three-fold increase in the level of vehicle patrol had no measurable impact on crime, whether measured by victim surveys or by police statistics. Whilst there is some question whether the experimental conditions were successfully maintained, the most probable explanation of the findings is that people – including potential offenders – simply failed to notice increases in patrol strength of this size. Further studies in Newark (again carried out by the US Police Foundation) and in Flint, Michigan[11] similarly found that introducing or withdrawing foot patrols from an area did not affect crime levels.

An earlier but much less publicised British study, the Beat Patrol Experiment[12] found broadly consistent results, on the basis of police statistics alone. The study suggested that provided that there was some level of patrol, the precise level of patrol seemed not to affect recorded crime rates. Further weight was added to these conclusions by a much quoted Home Office estimate[13] of the probability (in 1983) of a uniformed patrol officer intercepting a burglar:

> Given burglary rates and evenly distributed patrol coverage, a patrolling policeman in London could expect to pass within 100 yards of a burglary in progress roughly once every eight years – but not necessarily to catch the burglar or even realise that the crime was taking place.

In deriving this estimate, we made some questionable assumptions, particularly that patrols were robotic (or literally random) in their patrolling tactics; but even allowing for a rather more intelligent approach to the job, it was clear that routine patrols could pose only a small risk of arrest to most offenders.

Studies of intensive patrol activity targeted on crime 'hotspots' has yielded much less pessimistic results. Intensive patrolling has been shown to reduce crime, certainly for as long as the intensive activity continues, in a variety of settings ranging from shopping centres and housing estates to car parks and railway stations and street drug markets.[14] These studies demonstrate that once patrol strength has reached a critical mass which is obvious to offenders, the latter will respond accordingly, and curb their offending. What is less clear is the extent of displacement of offending over place, time and type of offence. It is obviously methodologically complex (to say the least) to demonstrate that crimes committed at one particular place and time would have been committed elsewhere under different circumstances. In almost all settings a degree of displacement can be expected; but it is unlikely that intensive patrolling ever results in 100 per cent displacement. The challenge is to find the best trade-off between the duration (and thus cost) of intensive patrol, the geographical coverage of patrol and the extent of displacement.[15]

Rapid response

With the advent of mobile patrols and computer-aided despatching systems in the 1970s it was hoped that rapid response to calls for police help would create a sense of police omni-presence, thus generating a deterrent effect. Both British and American research poured cold water on fast response as a strategy for tackling crime.[16] It was found that only a very small proportion of calls for police help involved crimes in progress, and that even where this was the case, offenders generally required seconds rather than minutes to make good their escape. In other words, the research demonstrated that fast response was inevitably unproductive in terms of arrests – though it never sought to examine the broader impact of consistently fast response to each and every call for police help. Like most propositions positing general deterrent effects, the thesis has never been fully tested empirically.

A decade later, it seems astonishingly profligate even to contemplate a blanket strategy of rapid response to all calls, regardless of their intrinsic urgency. Formal or informal systems of graded response are now commonplace; the essence of these is to preserve the capacity for rapid response in those situations where it is really required. Thus the Metropolitan Police Policing Plan for 1995/96, for example, has as a key objective, 'to respond promptly to emergency calls from the public', and a related performance indicator – but no commitment to rapid response to non-emergency calls. Strategies such as this have the backing of research which has shown that for the majority of calls for police help, the caller is less concerned with speed of response, and more concerned that he or she should be given a clear indication of when the patrol will arrive, and that this expectation should actually be met.

Fear of crime and the policing of disorder

The foot patrol experiments in Newark and Flint[11] found that even if patrols had no impact on crime, they were welcomed by residents and seemed to have reduced anxiety about crime. At a time when it was widely thought that 'fear of crime' was a problem in its own right, only loosely linked to actual levels of crime, the discovery that patrols could reduce fear was taken up enthusiastically by criminal justice politicians and managers. The US Police Foundation conducted a further detailed evaluation of several fear-reducing strategies, set in Houston and Newark, which found that policing styles which maximised positive contact between police and public could reduce fear of crime. A similar study in this country found that such strategies increased public confidence in the police, though it failed to identify any impact on fear.[17]

Reducing fear of crime has now been adopted by many British police forces as a policing objective, ironically at a time when criminologists are no longer so ready to declare fear of crime 'a problem in its own right'.[18] However, there remains a persuasive research-based argument for persisting with strategies of fear reduction. The so-called 'Broken Windows' argument proposed by James Q. Wilson and George Kelling[19] suggests that certain levels of criminal and sub-criminal disorder (e.g. the presence of rowdy youths, drunks, public drug-use, tramps, vandalism and graffiti, and prostitution) can set up a spiral of neighbourhood decline, with increased fear of crime, migration of the law-abiding out of the area, weakening of informal social control and ultimately increases in serious crime. Wilson and Kelling argue for the policing of such 'incivilities' by permanently assigned foot patrols, with a view to breaking the vicious cycle in which fear of crime forms a part. Whilst the Broken Windows thesis raises difficult issues about the tolerance of social diversity, it provides a more convincing rationale for 'putting bobbies back on the beat' than fear reduction as a goal in its own right.

Community or neighbourhood policing

Whilst there had been plenty of advocates of 'communal' policing in the 1970s, the riots of the early 1980s, and Lord Scarman's report on them, undoubtedly helped raise community or neighbourhood policing up the policy agenda. Community policing has some obvious resonances with 'Broken Windows'-type policing, but some important differences. It shares the objective of empowering communities, and of sustaining or strengthening informal mechanisms of social control; but it places more emphasis on achieving public consensus and consent to policing within heterogeneous – and often ethnically diverse – communities.

At its most debased, community policing involves little more than a more skilful and self conscious handling of public relations. More intelligent variants recognise that bolstering police legitimacy involves more than the stage-management of appearances. Common themes in community policing approaches include allocating officers (or teams of officers) long-term to beats or sectors, maximising positive contact with the public, and identifying what local people regard as policing problems and priorities.[20]

Perhaps the most thorough-going example of neighbourhood policing in the 1980s was a series of trials set in London and Surrey – the evaluation of which was complicated by problems of 'implementation failure'.[21]

Sector policing and problem-oriented policing

Problem-oriented policing enjoys considerable popularity in the United States, where it is particularly closely associated with the work of Herman Goldstein.[22] The ideas, but not the label, have begun to establish themselves in British policing, usually under the label of sector policing.[23] Problem-oriented policing counts as a close relative of community policing, in that its concerns are partly to improve police accountability and responsiveness to local circumstances, and thus their legitimacy. But problem-oriented policing is also premised on the idea that conventional policing is overly-reactive, and fails to tackle the roots of the problems to which uniform patrols are deployed (often with monotonous regularity). Emphasis is placed on accurate identification of problems, and their formal analysis with a view to developing long-term solutions. An organisational consequence of this perspective is that patrol officers are usually allocated long term to a narrowly defined territory (as in community policing), to maximise their understanding of local problems; and they are given responsibility for problem identification and the development of solutions. There have been several positive evaluations in the US specifically of the problem-oriented approach, the most recent being by the Chicago Policing Evaluation Consortium.[24] There has also been some research in England: the Metropolitan Police Service's system of sector policing, which is grounded in the ideas of problem-oriented policing, has received some evaluation,[23] and research is in progress in the Thames Valley Police Force area.

The strength of problem-oriented policing lies in the way in which it combines a rational problem-solving approach to day-to-day patrol work with the insights of community policing about the need to foster police accountability, responsiveness and legitimacy. Its limits may lie in the limited tractability of many of the problems which lead to calls for police assistance, or at least the limits to police competencies in tackling them. If Bittner's analysis stands up, what marks the police apart from other agencies of local government is precisely their ability to deal with any emergency which may require the use of force. The more that they are required to tackle not only the emergency but the underlying problem that created the emergency, the broader their mandate becomes, and the heavier their workload. This does not constitute a fatal flaw to the problem-oriented approach, but it implies both the importance of efficient cooperation between different local authority agencies, and the need to establish where the boundaries lie between policing and, for example, public health, housing departments and social services.

Surveillance technology

Over the last two years there has been a surge of popular support for closed circuit television (CCTV) as a supplement to the surveillance offered by uniformed patrols. Considerable claims have been made about the crime preventive impact of CCTV, but there is little properly conducted work assessing the impact in the target area, the extent of displacement and the extent of 'habituation effects' (as the novelty of the technology wears off). As ever with technology, it is more likely to yield a return the more it is conceived of as a *support* for human activity rather than a *substitute* for it.

The drive for efficiency

Finally, something should be said about the considerable pressures on the police for greater efficiency, best exemplified by the 1993 Audit Commission report.[25] Despite its subtitle, 'Tackling crime effectively', its preoccupation was less with 'what works' in policing and more with improving efficiency. Some of the best practice it commended is now becoming more widespread: better integration between the uniformed branch and CID, with more sharply defined roles and responsibilities for each; transferring the investigation of less serious crime from the CID to the uniformed branch; the setting-up of crime desks and crime management units to ensure more efficient handling of work; and the targeting of persistent offenders. It remains to be seen how substantial an impact targeting of this sort has on crime – though experience from Operation Bumblebee and similar operations is promising.[26]

Conclusions

A great deal of research on the police has been carried out over the last twenty five years. Much of it has been in North America, and there may be some limits to its applicability here. Collectively, however, the studies offered a critique of the dominant view of policing in the 1960s, which posited a fairly simple and mechanistic relationship between police activity and crime rates. The findings have helped to define (or redefine) the competencies of the uniformed police in tackling crime.

Part of the research message is with the *limits* on policing as a means of controlling crime. Many studies show that the uniformed police have a substantially limited capability for crime control; they imply that simply putting more uniformed police officers on the streets will yield few immediate pay-offs in terms of crime reduction. On a more positive note, however, research provides some support for those policing philosophies which emphasise the interdependence of formal and informal systems of social control, and the need to sustain police legitimacy. Policing strategies which reduce fear of crime and increase public satisfaction with the police may yield longer term pay-offs – even if evaluations have not managed to identify any immediate impact on crime rates. Research also offers some support to styles of policing which emphasise a rational problem solving approach in tackling local problems of crime and disorder.

References

1. Gorer, G. (1955) *Exploring British Character*. London: Cresset.
    Reiner, R. (1994) Policing and the police. In Maguire, M., Morgan, R. and Reiner, R. (eds) *The Oxford Handbook of Criminology*. Oxford: Clarendon Press.

2. Punch, M. and Naylor, T. (1973) The police: a social service. *New Society*, 24, pp 358-361.
    Comrie, M. and Kings, E. (1974) *Study of Urban Workloads: final report*. Home Office Police Research Services Unit. (Unpublished)
    Punch, M. (1979) The secret social service. In Holdaway, S. (ed) *The British Police*. London: Edward Arnold.
    McCabe, M. and Sutcliffe, S. (1978) *Defining Crime: a Study in Police Decision Making*. Oxford: Blackwell.
    Hough, J.M. (1980) *Uniformed Police Work and Management Technology*. Home Office Research Unit Paper No. 1. London: Home Office.
    Clarke, R.V.G. and Hough, J.M. (eds) (1980) *The Effectiveness of Policing*. Farnborough: Gower.

3. Banton, M. (1964) *The Policeman in the Community*. London: Tavistock.

4. Bittner, E. (1970) *The Function of the Police in Modern Society*. Washington, DC: United States Government Printing Office. (Republished 1975 by James Ronson, N.Y.)

   Bittner, E. (1974) Florence Nightingale in pursuit of Willie Sutton: a theory of the police. In Jacob, H. (ed) *The Potential for Reform in Criminal Justice*. Beverly Hills: Sage.

5. Reiss, A. (1971) *The Police and Public*. New Haven: Yale University Press.

   Mawby, R. (1979) *Policing the City*. Farnborough: Gower.

   Bottomley, A. and Coleman, C. (1981) *Understanding Crime Rates*. Farnborough: Gower.

   Burrows, J. (1982) How crimes come to police notice. *Research Bulletin No. 13*, 12-15. London: Home Office.

6. Cain, M.E. (1973) *Society and the Policeman's Role*. London: Routledge and Kegan Paul.

   Chatterton, M. (1979) Police in social control. In King, J. (ed) *Control Without Custody*. Cropwood Papers, University of Cambridge Institute of Criminology.

   Manning, P.K. (1977) *Police Work: The Social Organisation of Policing*. Cambridge, Mass: MIT Press.

7. Mayhew, P., Mirrlees-Black, C. and Aye Maung, N. (1994) *Trends in Crime: Findings from the 1994 British Crime Survey*. Research Findings No. 14. London: Home Office.

8. Barclay, G.C. (ed) (1993). *Digest 2: Information on the Criminal Justice System in England and Wales*. London: Home Office.

9. Reiner, R. (1994). Policing and the Police. In Maguire, M., Morgan, R. and Reiner, R. (eds) *The Oxford Handbook of Criminology*. Oxford: Clarendon Press.

10. Kelling, G., Pate, T., Dieckman, D. and Brown, C. (1974). *The Kansas City Preventive Patrol Experiment*. Washington, DC: Police Foundation.

11. Police Foundation (1981) *The Newark Foot Patrol Experiment*. Washington DC: Police Foundation.

    Trojanowicz, R.C. (1986) Evaluating a neighbourhood foot patrol program. In Rosenbaum, D.P. (ed) *Community Crime Prevention: does it work?* London: Sage.

12. Bright, J.A. (1969) *The Beat Patrol Experiment*. Home Office Police Research and Development Branch. (Unpublished)

13. Clarke, R.V.G. and Hough, J.M. (eds) (1984) *Crime and Police Effectiveness*. Home Office Research Study Number 79. London: HMSO.

14. Sherman, L.W. (1990) Police crackdowns: initial and residual deterrence. In Tonry, M. and Morris, N. (eds) *Crime and Justice: A Review of Research*. Volume 12. Chicago: University of Chicago Press.

15. Hesseling, R. (1994) Displacement: a review of the empirical literature. In Clarke, R.V.G. (ed) *Crime Prevention Studies*. Volume 3. Monsey NY: Criminal Justice Press.

16. Bieck, W. (1977) *Response Time Analysis*. Kansas City Police Department.

    Spelman, W. and Brown, D. (1981) *Calling the Police: Citizen Reporting of Serious Crime*. Washington, DC: Police Executive Research Forum.

    Ekblom, P. and Heal, K. (1982) *The Police Response to Calls from the Public*. Research and Planning Unit Paper No. 9. London: Home Office.

17. Pate, A.M., Wycoff, M.A., Skogan, W.G. and Sherman, L.W. (1986) *Reducing Fear of Crime in Houston and Newark*. Washington DC: Police Foundation.
    Bennett, T. (1991) The effectiveness of a police-initiated fear reducing strategy. *British Journal of Criminology*, 31, pp 1-14.

18. Hough, J.M. (1995) *Anxiety about Crime: Findings from the 1994 British Crime Survey*. Home Office Research Study No. 147. London: Home Office.

19. Wilson, J.Q. and Kelling, G.L. (1982) Broken windows. *The Atlantic Monthly*, March, 29-38.
    Skogan, W.G. (1990) *Disorder and Decline: Crime and the Spiral of Decay in American Neighbourhoods*. New York: Free Press.

20. Weatheritt, M. (1983) Community policing: does it work and how do we know? A review of research. In Bennett, T. (ed) *The Future of Policing*. Cropwood Conference Series No. 15. Cambridge: Institute of Criminology.
    Weatheritt, M. (1986) *Innovations in Policing*. London: Croom Helm.

21. Turner, P. (1987) *Evaluation of Neighbourhood Policing: Overall Report*. London: Metropolitan Police
    Irving, B., Bird, C., Hibberd, M. and Willmore, J. (1989) *Neighbourhood Policing: The Natural History of a Policing Experiment*. London: Police Foundation.

22. Goldstein, H. (1979) Improving policing: a problem-oriented approach. *Crime and Delinquency*, 25, pp 236-258.
    Goldstein, H. (1990) *Problem Oriented Policing*. Philadelphia: Temple University Press.

23. Dixon, B. and Stanko, E. (1993) *Serving the People: Sector Policing and Public Accountability*. London: Islington Council.

24. Chicago Community Policing Evaluation Consortium (1995) *Community Policing in Chicago, Year Two: an interim report*. Chicago: Illinois Criminal Justice Information Authority.

25. Audit Commission (1993) *Helping with Enquiries: Tackling Crime Effectively*. London: HMSO.

26. Stockdale, J.E. and Gresham, P. (1995) *Combating Burglary: An Evaluation of Three Strategies*. Police Research Group Crime Prevention and Detection Series. London: HMSO.

Public Opinion and the Police

Wesley G. Skogan

Summary

- The use of surveys of public attitudes to monitor the performance of the police and to set policing priorities is limited by which questions are asked and how they are framed, particularly with regard to issues about which most people have little direct experience.

- Surveys between 1982 and 1988 found that public confidence in the police declined even amongst groups that have traditionally been most supportive. By 1992 general satisfaction with the police had not risen above the 1988 level.

- People who have had contacts with the police, either by reporting an incident or by being stopped, are more likely to be satisfied with the police response if they were kept informed of any action taken, feel they were treated politely and fairly, and that the police were interested in what they said.

- People are more satisfied with the police, and are likely to be less fearful of crime, the more police they see on foot patrol.

- In setting operational priorities, the public want the police to focus on traditional crime concerns, by dealing with serious violence, burglary and vehicle related thefts, and to come quickly when called.

- The priorities set by the public for the police may not fit with limited resources.

Introduction

Surveys of public opinion and experience of crime and the police have become an integral part of the rapid change now sweeping through policing. The Victims Charter and the Citizens Charter both emphasise the need for customer-client relationships in the public sector including the police. The Audit Commission has outlined a list of workload and performance measures to be published by each police force.[1] Alterations are being proposed to police organisation and management that are intended to fix greater responsibility for decision making closer to the point where officers meet the public. The Association of Chief Police Officers (ACPO) notes that people rightly expect 'the highest possible standard of fairness, courtesy and sensitivity in the behaviour of officers with whom they come into contact...'[2]

Surveys of the general public are playing an increasing role in monitoring and guiding these shifts toward greater police accountability to the public. Many have been national in scope, but local forces are also conducting surveys to gauge public views of what actions they should take, and what happens when they do. Not all of the news that comes from these surveys is good. During the 1980s the British Crime Survey (BCS) and other national surveys documented a clear decline in public satisfaction with the police, and in respect for the occupation. Some local force surveys point to the same conclusion, often documenting disproportionate declines in satisfaction with policing among racial minorities. Trust in the police has declined, as has confidence in the legal system generally.[3,4]

Trends in general satisfaction

The BCS found that the percentage of people who rated the performance of their local police as 'very good' dropped from 43 per cent in 1982 to 25 per cent in 1988.[5] The widespread nature of this decline was perhaps as important as its magnitude. Compared with earlier surveys the 1988 BCS found confidence in the police had declined among broad categories of people who in the past had been most generally supportive. These included women, the elderly, whites, and residents of small towns and rural areas. Between December 1990 and October 1992 six national surveys, and the 1992 BCS, point to a stabilisation of confidence in the police during 1990-92 at or just below the 1988 BCS level, with between 23 per cent and 27 per cent of people rating the police as 'very good'.[6,7]

These trends are mirrored in local surveys. Surveys since 1984 in some Metropolitan Police divisions revealed that the percentage of London residents saying that the police in their area 'do a very good job' drifted down from 18 per cent to 15 per cent, fuelled in the main by decreasing levels of satisfaction among Afro-Caribbeans.[8,9,10,11]

National surveys by MORI, which simply ask people if they are satisfied or dissatisfied with 'the way your area is policed', also indicate a drop in satisfaction at about the same period. In 1981 75 per cent were satisfied, in 1985 67 per cent and in 1987 59 per cent. By January 1993 the percentage who were satisfied had drifted down to 51 per cent, but then rebounded to 59 per cent later in the year.[3,4] Between April 1989, and January 1994 the percentage who agreed with the statement 'I feel I can trust the police' declined from 75 per cent to 66 per cent.[4]

Specific sources of satisfaction and dissatisfaction

While general patterns of satisfaction with policing – and especially their trend – may be informative, it is probably more useful to examine the views of the public concerning specific features of policing. There are two general approaches to this task. The first is to present respondents with lists of various police activities or functions, and ask how satisfied they are with them. The second is to examine actual experiences that people have with the police to determine what features of those contacts satisfy or dissatisfy them. Both approaches can be illustrated with findings from the 1992 BCS, the most recent to be published.[7]

Views of police activities

The 1992 BCS gave respondents a long list of police activities, and asked how good a job police in their area made of each of them. Overall, the police were thought to do a particularly good job at dealing with crowds, serious motoring offences, and accidents. They received middling scores for their handling of rowdy, loutish and drunken behaviour and in their ability to keep traffic flowing smoothly.

The public had very mixed opinions about routine police patrolling. Twenty per cent thought they did a very good job at vehicular patrol but were much less satisfied with foot patrol: only 8 per cent thought they did a very good job, 29 per cent thought they did a fairly poor job, and 32 per cent a very poor job. In general, big-city residents and people who were worried about crime were more likely to be dissatisfied with patrolling. There was a strong correlation between how satisfied people were with both types of police patrols and remembering having seen an officer recently on foot patrol, a finding that has been replicated in several local force surveys.

Fighting crime

The public ranks burglary as one of the most serious crimes but the Gallup surveys found that public confidence in the ability of the police to solve burglaries dropped between 1983 and 1992.[12] Respondents to the 1992 BCS gave a low rating to police effectiveness in controlling burglary, only 8 per cent thought they did a very good job.

The BCS respondents scored police somewhat higher on their capacity to deal with violent crime, with 21 per cent saying they did a very good job. The Gallup surveys found that public confidence in this aspect of police performance has been stable since 1983.

Relations with the community

Police received middling marks from the 1992 BCS respondents for the way they handled crime prevention advice: 25 per cent thought they did a very good job. Considerably fewer thought they did a very good job in proffering aid to victims, 13 per cent, and in their ability to work with community groups, 14 per cent.

Comment

One difficulty with these survey-based performance measures is that inevitably there are many aspects of police activity about which ordinary citizens are uninformed. They often know little about how the police are organised and what they are doing, much less how well they are doing it, and in the absence of any direct experience their views of policing are importantly shaped by the mass media.[5] In the BCS, and other surveys, substantial percentages of respondents indicate that they do not know how good a job the police do at particular tasks. 'Don't know' responses were more common among people who had little recent experience with crime or the police, while victims and those who had contacted the police or had been stopped by an officer were much more likely to have an opinion.

Public contacts with the police

Asking people who have had contact with the police to rate the performance of police officers on some fairly specific criteria can reveal experiential factors that are systematically linked to satisfaction with specific encounters, suggesting which aspects of police behaviour are shaping public opinion. In the BCS respondents are quizzed to determine if they have had any contact with the police during the year preceding the interview. If they have, they are asked a sequence of detailed questions about the encounter, and provided with rating scales on which they can register how satisfied they were with the police handling of the matter.

Contacts initiated by the public

The 1992 BCS showed the greatest pool of discontentment with the police was among people who contacted them to report a crime; about one-third were dissatisfied with how police handled their case, as were about 20 per cent who had reported a potential crime (for example, a disturbance, a ringing alarm or a suspicious circumstance). Those contacting the police to ask for information or to give them information were generally pleased with how they were received.

Four factors stood out as important determinants of satisfaction with encounters people had initiated with the police:

Being kept informed. Only one quarter of crime victims or reporters of potential crimes felt they were kept informed about their case by the police, by a large margin their biggest complaint.

Being treated politely. About 70 per cent of those contacting the police said that they thought they were treated very politely, and very few thought police were actually impolite. However, Afro-Caribbeans and (especially) Asians, were disproportionately dissatisfied with how their encounter was handled.

Appropriate levels of effort. Only about two-thirds of crime victims thought police gave their case as much effort as they should have, and only slightly more of those reporting a potential crime thought so.

Police interested in their story. About 70 per cent of those reporting a crime felt the police paid sufficient attention to what they had to say. Among those who did not feel this, three-quarters were dissatisfied with how the police handled their case.

These findings suggest that new measures to keep people informed about what happened as a result of their contact would pay significant dividends in terms of rebuilding public confidence in the police. The effort the police put into many cases goes unobserved by the general public, and finding ways to bring those efforts to public notice would both keep people informed and reassure them that there is real interest in tackling the problems they face. The report on policing from the 1988 BCS called for new efforts to refocus officers' attention on the importance of the care and aid that they dispense, along with rewarding their technical proficiency, in order to speak to the concerns of the public.[5]

Contacts initiated by the police

Sixteen per cent of the 1992 BCS respondents had been involved in vehicular stops by the police, and 3 per cent had been stopped while on foot. There was little dissatisfaction with routine vehicle stops: most drivers were given reasons for being stopped, few were searched, and most escaped without formal sanction. People who were stopped on foot were more dissatisfied, perhaps because of the more ambiguous circumstances under which many pedestrian stops took place. More often the stops were for reasons that people thought were unrelated to an offence, the police less frequently gave reasons for the stop, and they made more searches. But at the same time, perhaps because they were less routinised, officers actually paid more attention to what people stopped had to say and few were arrested or otherwise sanctioned.

The factors most closely linked to satisfaction with the outcomes of such encounters with the police were being treated fairly and politely, and perceiving that the officers showed interest in what the targets of their stops had to say. Perhaps inevitably, pedestrian stops seemed more unfair and the officers involved in them were viewed as more impolite. In general, it was young, single, unemployed Afro-Caribbean men who were more frequently the targets of stops of all kinds, and who were more likely to feel that they were treated unfairly.

Priorities for the police

Surveys may ask respondents to set priorities for the police by asking 'What are the most important *problems* for police to concentrate on?'[14,15,16] or by examining public support for specific kinds of police *activities*. In a typical example of the first approach, the survey conducted as part of the Operational Policing Review gave respondents a list of problems and asked them to select up to five offences they thought 'the police should spend most time and energy trying to fight'.[13]

Problems

It is important to note that the nature of the problems listed, and how the questions are phrased, help to frame the conclusions that can be drawn from a survey. The survey for the Operational Policing Review[13] presented respondents with a broad range of problems to choose from, including 'litter and rubbish lying around' as well as street robbery, but other lists might not be so inclusive. When asked about priorities for police action the candidate problems was all described as 'offences'. Whether or not a particular problem fell within what the respondent considered to be the legitimate concern of the police was determined by the interviewer. If allowed to make up their own minds respondents may have come to different conclusions.

In a survey in Sussex[16], respondents were presented with a list of problems and asked 'should the police deal with them?' While there was some variation, responses largely fell into three categories: a long list of conventional policing problems, which mostly drew 'yes' responses regardless of their seriousness or frequency; a shorter list of environmental problems outside the limits of the traditional police mandate (for example, 'litter'), which mostly drew 'no' responses; and a few traffic regulation issues (for example, 'heavy lorries') which fell in-between. This and other surveys suggest that the public put traffic control low on their agenda for the police.

The surveys which have asked 'which important problems the police should concentrate on' indicate a fair degree of consensus about the main concerns: sexual assaults and burglary ranked highest followed by drunk-driving, vandalism and robbery. There was, however, no direct relationship between how common people thought these problems were and the priority they gave them. For example, in West Mercia respondents were asked if each problem on the list happened a great deal, a fair amount, not very much, or not at all.[14] Sexual assaults and drunk-driving were ranked among the least frequently occurring problems, but were among the top priorities for police attention. The most common offences (dog fouling, rubbish and litter, parking offences) were ranked very low as priorities. On the other hand, burglary, vandalism and vehicle-related thefts were highly rated concerns *and* were considered to be fairly common problems, a juxtaposition of opinions that might be taken seriously in priority setting.

However, it is important to recognise that the nature of local problems varies considerably from place to place, as well as from time to time. There is tremendous inter-area variation in the type, intensity, and mix of local problems, and many of them display a marked seasonal pattern. The fact of this extensive variation is one reason for recommending local force surveys to use large enough samples to speak to differences among important sub-areas.

For example, a 1994 survey for the Greater Manchester Police[17] involved interviewing 100 people (not a very large sample) in each of the 13 divisions of the force. It found that the percentage of residents rating 'burglary and theft' the 'single most serious problem' in their area ranged from 2 per cent to 22 per cent. The range for 'street crime' was from less than 1 per cent to 22 per cent, car crime 13 per cent to 28 per cent, and 'young people hanging/driving around' from 5 per cent to 24 per cent. People who were most concerned about burglary in their area tended to give a low ranking to street crime, and *vice versa*. A survey in North Wales also found much local variation.[18]

Surveys *might* be able to document unanticipated trends in public concern, if appropriate response categories are included. For example, the surveys for the Metropolitan Police identified a tremendous surge of concern about car crime, beginning in the early 1990s so that among London residents it now stands above vandalism and mugging as the most important problem in their area. Public surveys usually rely on pre-established questions and pre-coded response categories (for ease and speed of completion and to keep the costs down) so that they are a more useful tool for confirming ideas than for discovering them.

Police activities

The high affection the public has for foot patrol can be found in all the national and local surveys reviewed here. In many police areas foot patrol may be ranked in priority even above responding quickly to 999 calls, and is often ranked above investigating crimes and detecting and arresting offenders. Of course, it is likely that respondents think that foot patrol would improve police capabilities in these matters but the gap between the level of priority given to foot patrol and car patrol – which does not have much support – indicates there is something particularly appealing about foot patrol. Responding to 999 calls also garners a high level of support, for example, immediate response to 999 calls was the highest priority of Islington residents.[19] The high ranking given to the police 'getting to know people' also points to a great desire on the part of the public for more 'hands on' policing that responds to the needs of the local community.

In the surveys the visibility of police officers on foot patrol is highly correlated with general measures of satisfaction with policing, with satisfaction with local levels of foot patrol and with reduced fear of crime especially of street crime and vandalism.

The 1992 BCS found that 7 per cent of respondents recalled having seen a police officer patrolling on foot very recently ('today or yesterday'), and about 20 per cent within the past week. Foot patrols were more visible in inner city and metropolitan areas throughout England and Wales, and especially in inner London. Whites and Asians were likely to attribute positive effects to visible foot patrol. Afro-Caribbeans (and young men) most frequently recalled seeing an officer on foot, but – mirroring their generally less satisfactory encounters with them – visible foot patrol had no reassuring effects among these two groups.[7]

Comment

One reason for being cautious about the use of surveys in setting priorities is that they can make it very easy for the public to request 'more' of almost everything without counting the cost or considering the different kind of resources required to deal with different problems. For example, a survey in early 1994 found that 87 per cent of the public wanted 'more police on the beat'.[4]

Another reason for being cautious about the role of surveys in setting operational priorities is that a large proportion – some think too large a proportion – of the police agenda is reactive, set in response to 999 calls and other incidents as they occur. In this sense the public is *already* setting priorities for the police, and controlling a significant percentage of their resources.

Many police forces have been experimenting with schemes to match some requests for service with alternative modes of response or by diverting them to other agencies. These graded response policies are a tactical reaction to mounting police workloads, and they have been justified in part by the large fraction of calls which are of a non-emergency, non-crime character. There might be some role for opinion research on priorities for load shedding, but the bulk of the candidate incidents (for example, long-completed burglaries or accidents not posing a threat to life) have not so far been included in surveys of public priorities for policing.

Conclusions

There are limits to the use of public surveys as guides to making policy with regard to policing, and this is particularly true of hypothetical questions about which the respondents have little direct experience. Surveys are most appropriately a guide to policy when they focus on things with which most people have had direct experience, but for many of the general public this excludes important aspects of policing.

The public image of the police that emerges from the surveys reviewed here is one that wants them to focus on traditional crime concerns like serious violent crimes, burglary, and vehicle-related thefts. They want the police to come rapidly when called. At the same time, they want more direct 'hands on' contact with the police. In my judgement, the popularity of foot patrol is probably based on how it bridges these two quite different concerns.

The surveys also signal public concern that local forces are not responding as quickly as they might to calls for assistance. The Joint Consultative Committee's report found both that responding rapidly to calls should be a high priority *and* that three-quarters of all respondents thought that all crimes deserve equal attention. Clearly this is an unrealistic juxtaposition.

Likewise, the issue of foot patrol highlights the potential clash between popular and administrative concerns. Foot patrol is expensive to mount, it is often in competition for staffing with other highly-rated activities (like responding quickly to 999 calls), and it does not score highly on traditional police performance indices such as making arrests and clearing up crimes. Foot patrol presents a hard set of choices for police forces pressed on one side to reduce costs and control the growth of personnel, and on the other to respond to the expectations of the public.

References

1. Market Opinion Research International (1993) *Police Performance Indicators*. Research study conducted for the Audit Commission. London: MORI.

2. Association of Chief Police Officers (1990) *Setting the Standards for Policing: Meeting Community Expectations*. London: ACPO.

3. Market Opinion Research International (1993) *Public Attitudes to the Police*. Research study conducted for the *Sunday Times* and the Police Federation. London: MORI.

4. Market Opinion Research International (1994) *Public Attitudes to Crime*. Research study conducted for the Readers Digest Magazine. London: MORI.

5. Skogan, W.G. (1990) *The Police and Public in England and Wales*. Home Office Research Study No. 117. London: HMSO.

6. Southgate, P. and Crisp, D. (1992) *Public Satisfaction with Police Services*. Research and Planning Unit Paper No. 73. London: Home Office.

7. Skogan, W.G. (1994) *Contacts Between Police and Public: Findings from the 1992 British Crime Survey*. Home Office Research Study No. 134. London: HMSO.

8. Social and Community Planning Research (1984) *The Police and the Community in Brixton Division*. A Report for the Metropolitan Police. London: SCPR.

9. Social and Community Planning Research (1985) *The Police and the Community in Kilburn Division*. A Report for the Metropolitan Police. London: SCPR.

10. Market Opinion Research International (1993) *Richmond Residents' Attitudes to Policing*. Research Study conducted for the Richmond Division of the Metropolitan Police. London: MORI.

11. Metropolitan Police and London Borough of Hounslow (1994) *Survey of Local Residents*. London: Quality Assurance Unit, Metropolitan Police.

12. Gallup Ltd. (1992) *Political and Economic Index*. Report 386. London: Gallup Ltd.

13. Joint Consultative Committee (1990) *The Operational Policing Review*. Surbiton: Joint Consultative Committee of the three Police Staff Associations of England and Wales.

14. Harris Research Centre (1991) *Policing in West Mercia*. Richmond: Harris Research Centre.

15. Harris Research Centre (1992) *Public Attitude Survey for Hampshire Constabulary*. Richmond: Harris Research Centre.

16. Shapland, J., Wiles, P. and Leek, M. (1990) *Policing in Sussex: a Public Survey*. University of Sheffield: Centre for Criminological and Socio-Legal Studies.

17. Research Services Limited (1994) *A General Public Perception Survey Prepared for the Greater Manchester Police*. Harrow: Research Services Limited.

18. Waddon, A. and Baker, C. (1990) *Public Perceptions of the North Wales Police*. Bangor: University College of North Wales.

19. Jones, T., MacLean, B. and Young, J. (1986) *The Islington Crime Survey*. Aldershot: Gower.

Public and Private Policing

Clifford Shearing

Summary

- Since a professional state police was created by Sir Robert Peel in the early 19th century, policing has been seen as a service provided by the government to the public.

- Contemporary developments in community policing, and the growth of the market mentality, have resulted in policing becoming 'ruled at a distance' by the state, with individuals being made responsible for the business of policing.

- The growth of mass private property used by the public has resulted in corporate entities becoming 'private governments' employing private police in order to reduce loss.

- Policing for security by both state and private police has resulted in a shift in emphasis from fighting crime to loss prevention.

- The growth of private policing means that the state police can no longer dictate the direction of policing or their role in it.

- Initiatives in multi-tiered policing, with the state police engaging in partnerships with private police, social agencies and citizen volunteers, are being promoted in many countries to increase surveillance in public places in order to reduce opportunities for crime.

- A multi-tiered system of policing presents opportunities for restructuring policing that should be explored.

- Policy on multi-tiered policing must focus regulatory attention to the mobilisation of resources required to provide for security.

Introduction

Two sets of changes have been taking place in the location of the management of policing and both are the result of privatisation. What is privatised, however, is different. In the first case, with what I call the emergence of state 'rule at a distance', what is privatised is the business of policing. In the second, with the development of what I will refer to as 'private governments', what is privatised is both the business and the direction of policing.

State rule at a distance

The modern policing period was established in Britain in 1829, with the Metropolitan Police Act, when Sir Robert Peel initiated reforms designed to relocate the delivery of policing from the institutions of civil society to the state. For centuries before the Peelian reforms the business of policing had been the responsibility of local communities. An example of this is found in the institution of frankpledge where local responsibility to keep the royal peace was based on obligatory personal service by every male person and 'relied on the principle that all members of a community accepted an obligation for the good behaviour of each other'.[1] Under this system the role of the state, exercised through manorial courts, was primarily one of co-ordination and inspection to ensure that communities were undertaking policing activities, with local responsibility promoted through penalties levied against an individual or the whole community when they failed to keep the peace. Within this system rule took place 'at a distance'[2] with the Crown doing the 'steering' and the 'rowing' left to communities.[3]

In the late 18th century the twin developments of industrialisation and urbanisation changed the character of civil society in ways that made the system of local responsibility for policing less and less workable. This led to arguments for the establishment of a professional body of specialised officers who would undertake local policing. Under this strategy the state would both 'steer' and 'row'. The new police would need to have the trust and support of citizens to work effectively but it was they, rather than local people, who were to be responsible for policing. The public had been the police and the Peelian reforms were intended to do precisely the opposite, so that the new police were not the public and the public were not the police.

Peel's reforms created a professional state police and this concept has dominated policing since the mid-19th century. At its heart is an understanding that accords responsibility for policing to the state and defines citizens and communities as recipients of the service. While this understanding predated a Keynesian conception of governance, with its focus on state provision of services, it is consistent with it and was advanced and extended by the development of the welfare state.[4]

Policing became part of a wider Keynesian mode of governance and was seen as one of the services provided by the state through its agents thus extending and developing the Peelian dream of a state police responsible for keeping the peace. This conception is expressed in police mottos such as 'to serve and protect' (Metropolitan Toronto Police), and in arrangements that seek to enable people to reach out for policing services through the provision of emergency telephone numbers, and the emphasis on patrol and rapid response.

We are now entering a post-Keynesian era in which the role of the state is being challenged as part of a widespread movement to 're-invent government'.[5] This challenge is reflected within the domain of policing through initiatives, such as community policing, that seek to return responsibility for policing to citizens.[4] While this is a rebirth of older forms of policing it is not simply a return to the institutions of frankpledge. What is being reborn is a system of rule that uncouples the 'steering' and 'rowing' of policing and locates the responsibility for 'steering' with the state and for 'rowing' with citizens. This emerging arrangement is being conceptualised and promoted through metaphors such as 'partnership' that envision the state and citizens as allies in the quest for civil peace.

We are at present in the midst of a period of experimentation in which ways of accomplishing this uncoupling are being explored and 'best practice' is being identified and promoted. This process has redefined the role of the state police and has raised questions about the applicability of our established understanding of policing.

To understand the context in which these questions are being raised it is necessary to examine further the nature of the conception of 'rule at a distance' that is being explored in contemporary developments of community policing. Despite the rhetoric of 'communities' and 'community policing', it is not communities but individuals who are being made responsible for policing. The relationship envisaged is not between the state and communities, as was the case with frankpledge, but between the state and individuals. The new policing strategies seek to empower individuals to take responsibility for their lives.[6] Furthermore, within these developments the role of the state is primarily one of education rather than inspection, although there may be inspectorial elements.

At the nub of these changes is the market mentality and the market institutions that provide the context for the rebirth of 'rule at a distance' policing strategies. Such policing is conceived of in terms of 'customers' and 'commodities'. These metaphors reinforce the state-individual dichotomy and serve as the platform on which the shift is taking place from the logic and strategies of the welfare state with resonances of the situation before the Peelian reforms.

Private governments

In addition to state initiated developments of 'rule at a distance', a shift is occurring in the location of rule and steering, from public to private entities. This shift, which predates the move to rule at a distance governance identified above, can be explored through an examination of private policing which provides a useful lens through which to examine what Stuart Macauley[7] has termed 'private governments'.

Private governments exist both in a legal and illegal form. While illegal private governments, such as the warlords who control slum areas in places like South Africa and Brazil, constitute important features of contemporary governance in many parts of the world, my concern here is with legal private governments.

Private governments are associated with the shift of public life from public to private property – for instance, in shopping malls where public space is located on private property. A critical consequence of the emergence of 'mass private property' has been the development of private governments as corporate entities which have taken advantage of the provisions of property and contract law to regulate activities taking place on their property. Privately-owned and publically-used sites are policed by private security, with public and private police carrying out their duties on different geographical sites.[8]

Other examples of private government, or 'communities of governance', include such diverse collectivities as library users who agree through contracts to particular conditions, and 'gated communities', or more generally 'gated cities', where real estate law provides the basis for the construction of 'governance contracts'. These private governments deploy rule at a distance strategies that allocate the 'rowing' of governance, including policing, to others.

A critical feature of policing by private governments has been the development of private policing structures and practices that promote corporate security. It is often assumed that these developments have occurred because of inadequacies in state rule and that private policing, and private governance more generally, would disappear if state policing were more effective. This conception of private policing as filling a vacuum fails to recognise that private governments and the policing they undertake arise from developments that are far more fundamental than the problems associated with state policing. No matter how effective state policing becomes – either through the more effective use of police officers or through rule at a distance strategies – it is unlikely to have a major impact on the demand for private security from private governments.[9]

Policing for security

The Peelian proposals for policing reform involved a shift from 'bandit catching' (a term I owe to Jim Harding), with its focus on past breaches of the peace, to a mode of policing concerned with promoting security, rather than responding to insecurity. It is precisely this objective of promoting security that Lord Scarman[10] sought to resurrect when he argued that the police should give priority to 'the maintenance of public tranquillity' and the maintenance of 'the normal state of society' over the enforcement of the law.

Peel sought to establish a way of providing an 'unremitting watch' over the whole of London through the establishment of a professional specialised police force. For a variety of reasons, primarily to do with the 'institutions of privacy', Peel's new police and their offspring have had considerable difficulty in realizing this objective.[11] These difficulties have given rise to a whole series of initiatives to make the state police work in the way Peel had hoped with a central thrust being to get police officers to attend to problems more quickly in the hope that certainty of detection would deter would-be offenders. This, however, has had the effect of providing more, not less, bandit catching. Indeed, it can be argued that contemporary state policing, including the developments in community policing, is a direct response to the failure of the Peelian police to develop a future-oriented mode of policing that has the prevention of crime, not the response to crime, as its principal focus.[12]

The earliest and most far-reaching response to the failure of the Peelian dream can be found in developments within private governments and their policing. Indeed, it is precisely the Peelian dream of 'policing for security', as opposed to 'policing for law enforcement', that the rebirth of private security associated with private governments has sought to realise. This shift away from bandit-catching has manifested itself by a change of emphasis from fighting crime to loss prevention.

It is this change in focus from crime to loss, and from law enforcement to risk reduction, that unifies the developments in policing across the private-public divide. Both state governments and private governments are seeking to organise their policing in ways that will promote policing for security. This shared fulcrum provides the basis for relating the activities of public and private governments and public and private policing.

In considering the role of the police it is essential to think not simply of state governance but also of private governance and the relationship that is being forged, and that should be forged, between the two. A recognition of private government and its role in policing is necessary because it identifies the inadequacy of any framework of analysis that considers the state police as being in a position unilaterally to control and direct developments in policing. While this might have been true in the mid-twentieth century (although even this claim can be disputed) it is certainly not true today. The state police are not now in a position simply to dictate terms with respect to the direction of policing – they do not own it or their role in it.

To say this is not to deny that the shape of the regulatory space is defined at present by state law, and to an increasing degree, by suprastate law. These definitions (which arise out of contract law, labour law, property law etc.) reflect very widely held conceptions about the nature of the liberal state that are not likely to change significantly in the foreseeable future. It is this broader framework of values and regimes of law, that provide for regulatory spaces that include private governments as significant and independent players who engage in policing. While in principle the state could regulate policing in ways that would permit the state police to control the space in which it occurs, this is unlikely to happen in practice. The state police are simply not in a position to decide on their role, instead, what their role will be will depend on a continuing negotiation process.

Much has already taken place to articulate state and private policing and to re-define the role of the state police. At the nub of the changes have been the development of policing networks that include a variety of nodes including, but not limited to, the state. However, we know relatively little about these networks. Recently Richard Ericson[13] has provided an analysis that suggests that more and more state police time and resources are being deployed to service networks that have security rather than law enforcement as their principal objective. He argues that the police act as brokers in the collection and processing of information, for example, in relation to burglaries, which is used to promote the structures and procedures of insurance systems which operate to reduce risk by seeking to limit opportunities for loss.

Multi-tiered policing

The most direct evidence available at present on policing networks comes from initiatives to establish partnerships between the state police and other agencies. Initiatives designed to develop multi-tiered, or what might be better thought of as a networked approach to policing, can now be found in a variety of parts of the world. What unifies most of these approaches is that they seek to provide a network of policing resources that can be used to promote security policing.

Although multi-tiered initiatives are taking place globally much of the literature in English relates to North America and tends to focus on attempts by state police departments to promote networks. This does not mean that the police have been most active in building networks, rather that they are most likely to report on them. The initiatives have tended to be concerned with such questions as: what resources can be mobilised to assist the police in shifting from law enforcement to security, how should these resources be networked, what role should the police play in these networks.

The Oppal Report

The relationship between the state police and other policing resources was a particular focus in the report of a recent Canadian Commission, under the leadership of Mr Justice Oppal, which considered the future role of the state police in the province of British Columbia.[14]

The Oppal report notes, given the demands being made on the police, it is no longer feasible 'to expect the police to respond to all reports of offences or community problems' and that 'some types of law enforcement work can, and should be, done by non-police personnel such as civilians, private security firms or auxiliary officers'. The advocacy of multi-tiered policing is justified on the grounds that 'it reduces policing costs and frees highly trained police officers to respond to serious crimes where police are most needed'.

In arguing for greater civilian involvement in policing the report noted the regulated development that has already taken place. Civilian personnel are already used in some technical and administrative roles, to enforce by-laws, in victim assistance programmes, as special constables, as volunteer assistants in Neighbourhood Watch, with private security firms providing patrols, armoured car services and private investigations to communities and private individuals.

The Oppal report considered that multi-tiered policing had developed as a consequence of the requirements of community policing and noted that policing had become both networked and de-specialised. In considering the implications of multi-tiered policing the report recognised the dangers of 'too many cooks' and argued for some form of state co-ordination and oversight so that 'non-police personnel are properly accountable to the public'. The report also notes that non-police personnel need to be properly trained and that the allocation of duties to such personnel should not compromise public safety.

There have been surprisingly few thoughtful examinations of how the de facto tiering of policing that the emergence of private security has created should be managed and regulated. There have been several important descriptive studies that have identified the size and nature of the private security industry, and pointed to the necessity for its regulation and co-ordination[15] but little has been done to develop a framework for policing that seeks to co-ordinate and integrate private and state provision. What can be found are proposals that outline how police departments can enter into contracts with private security companies to engage in activities that do not require police powers.[16]

The Starrett City Experiment

The most thoroughly documented North American programme seeking to integrate and co-ordinate private and state policing resources is the Starrett City experiment. The Starrett City Reality Corporation, which owns the properties in this community, employs a private police department. The community exists within a high crime area in New York city but its crime rate is much lower than that of adjacent neighbourhoods. Research was carried out to determine whether this was attributable to the use of Starrett City's own security personnel.[17]

The security officers are agents of the property owners with unrestricted access to all areas and have full police powers. They can stop and challenge any person who is on Starrett City property and anyone who cannot provide a purpose for being there can be arrested for trespass. An examination of the tasks of the security officers found that they 'practise a highly visible proactive form of foot patrol that included service to residents ... and are considered an important part of the community who both serve and protect it'.

The net result is, the researchers argued, the institutionalisation of a style of community-oriented policing so that 'the merging of private interest, community need and policing style has created a positive crime prevention strategy'.

Other North American initiatives

Police departments across the United States are using a market approach to implement a problem-solving community policing style by building partnerships with resources that include, but are not limited to, volunteers and private security agencies. An example of the latter is the Security Watch programme in Philadelphia which 'utilises private security officers as the eyes and ears of the police department. The officers are trained by their agencies and the police department as to the type of information to be reported (of a non-emergency nature such as abandoned vehicles, sanitation violations etc) and how it is to be reported...'[18]

There is also a broad range of community policing programmes which focus on the recruitment of civilian volunteers into policing networks, such as Neighbourhood Watch, while others seek specifically to establish links with private security agencies. It has been argued that such links should be encouraged because 'like private security, community policing is proactive crime prevention that is accountable to the customer'.[19]

Programmes have also been developed to establish partnerships between the police and social agencies[20] and between different kinds of police agencies, for example, the US Naval Criminal Investigation Service.[21] A critical feature of these, as with many other partnerships, is the sharing of information.

The Dutch experience

A number of European countries have been exploring public-private police co-operation. Among the most developed are the initiatives in The Netherlands where a policy of crime prevention that seeks to promote networks of policing resources has been actively pursued for some time.[22] These initiatives with multi-tiered policing are promoted and subsidised by the government and, unlike North America, have not drawn upon established private sector provision. An important recent attempt to link public and private resources has been the establishment of a National Platform on Crime Control to encourage 'collaboration between government and the business world'.[23] As in the United States, the principal objective of these initiatives has been to promote better surveillance to reduce opportunities for crime.

Projects include the employment of 'city guards' (recruited from the long-term unemployed) in the inner cities to 'assist and inform the public, to observe all kinds of irregularities and report these to the proper authorities – either the police or a municipal service; and to prevent petty crime or other misbehaviour by surveillance'. Others involve 'controllers' on public transport (also recruited from the unemployed) and caretakers on public housing estates. Evaluations of these projects have shown a 'decrease in certain types of crime and a decrease in the feelings of insecurity of residents or the general public' as well as a decrease in the ranks of the unemployed.[24]

Critiques of the multi-tiered model

While most of the evaluations of initiatives in establishing multi-tiered forms of policing have tended to be supportive, especially in terms of public satisfaction, some critical comment can be found in the North American literature. For example, there have been cautions against generalizing from the Starrett City experiment because 'it may be the exception rather than the rule for proving the effectiveness of private security'.[25]

Central to these criticisms is the fear that private policing poses a threat to individual rights as a consequence of the absence of state regulation. That this can be remedied by seeking to establish a monopoly of state policing is, however, questioned by those who argue that it is too late to turn back from privatizing public justice – 'the crucial question is whether these changes will occur piecemeal and poorly or thoughtfully and well'.[26]

Conclusions

In my view, the critical issue to be addressed in considering the consequences of an increasing alignment of public and private resources is the possibility that a multi-tiered system of policing might exacerbate the duality that is already occurring within police departments between policing that seeks to promote compliance with a minimal recourse to force, and 'hard' policing that relies principally on the use of physical coercion. The danger here is the increasing isolation and militarisation of those units within police establishments that engage in hard policing. This possibility needs to be addressed in developing new institutional forms for policing. One example of how this may be done can be found in developments in public order policing in South Africa prior to that country's general election in 1994. As a result of a report by the Goldstone Commission a regulatory scheme was introduced which created alliances between hard and soft forms of policing. These alliances were structured to ensure that the use of force was under direct civilian control and that its use was integrated with less coercive forms of policing.[27]

What is required now is an exploration of both the concerns, and the possibilities, that the emergence of new policing institutions raise within a political climate that favours the decentralisation of governance. A central issue for serious consideration must be how policing for security should be resourced where it takes place through networks of institutions that extend beyond the state.

At present a host of governmental functions are funded by providing tax revenues to state institutions such as the police. This mode of provision assumes that these institutions 'own' governance – that the state police 'own' policing. What has become abundantly clear is that assumption is no longer valid. Policing, like governance generally, takes place in and through networks of public and private institutions. Any policy concerned with regulating policing requires proposals for resourcing that make security, and not the state police, their focus.

A shift from the funding of the state police to the funding of security requires a radical re-examination of the way in which tax revenues are allocated.[28] So long as these resources are allocated to the state police as the primary providers of security any proposals for regulating multi-tiered policing will be limited. As the saying goes, 'if you give a child a hammer everything begins to look like a nail'. Similarly, if the budget for security is given to the state police every security question begins to look like something that requires police attention. This issue of funding of security has to be addressed if a comprehensive policy on multi-tiered policing is to be developed.

References

1. Critchley, T. (1979) *A History of the Police in England and Wales.* (2nd edition) London: Constable.

2. Rose, N. and Miller, P. (1992) Political power beyond the state: problematics of government. *British Journal of Sociology*, 43, pp 173-205.

3. Savas, E.S. cited by Osbourne, D. and Gaebler, T. (1993) *Reinventing Government.* New York: Plume.

4. O'Malley, P. (1994) *Post-Keynesian Policing.* La Trobe University.

5. Osbourne, D. and Gaebler, T. (1993) *Reinventing Government.* New York: Plume.

6. Cruikshank, B. (1994) The will to empower: technologies of citizenship and the war on poverty. *Socialist Review*, 23, pp 29-55.

7. Macauley, S. (1986) Private government. In Lipson, L. and Wheeler, S. (eds) *Law and the Social Sciences.* New York: Russell Sage Foundation.

8. Marinos, V. (1994) *Challenging the Public-police Divide: Policing Student Behaviour in Ontario High Schools.* Toronto: Centre of Criminology, University of Toronto.

9. Shearing, C. (1992) The relationship between public and private policing. In Tonry, M. and Morris, N. (eds) *Modern Policing.* Chicago: University of Chicago Press. Johnston, L. (1992) *The Rebirth of Private Policing.* London: Routledge.

10. Scarman, Lord (1982) *The Brixton Disorders 10-12 April 1981. Report of an Inquiry.* London: HMSO.

11. Stinchcombe, A. (1963) Institutions of privacy in the determination of police administrative practices. *American Journal of Sociology*, 96, pp 150-160.

12. Shearing, C. (1995) Reinventing policing: policing as governance. In Sack, F. *et al.* (eds) *Privatisierung Staatlicher Kontrolle: Befunde, Kontrolle, Befunde, Konzepte, Tendenzen.* Baden Baden: Nomos Verslagsgellschaft.

13. Ericson, R., Haggerty, K. and Carriere, K. (1993) Community policing as communications policing. In Dolling, D. and Feltes, T. (eds) *Community Policing: Comparative Aspects of Community Oriented Police Work.* Holzkirchen: Felix Verlag.
Ericson, R. (1994) The division of expert knowledge in policing and security. *British Journal of Sociology*, 45, pp 149-175.

14. Oppal, W.T. (1994) *Closing the Gap: Policing and the Community.* The Report of Policing in British Columbia Commission of Inquiry.

15. Cunningham, W. and Taylor, T. (1985) *The Hallcrest Report: Private Security and Police in America.* Portland: Chancellor.

16. Chaiken, M. and Chaiken, J. (1987) *Public Policing – Privately Funded.* Washington D.C.: US Department of Justice.

17. Walsh, W.F. and Donovan, E.J. (1989) Private security and community policing: evaluation and comment. *Journal of Criminal Justice*, 17, pp 187-197.

18. Zappile, R.A. (1991) Philadelphia implements security watch. *The Police Chief*, 58 (August), pp 22-23.

19. Kolpacki, T. (1994) Neighbourhood Watch. *Security Management*, 36, pp 47-48.

20. Johnston, S. and Fancher, L. (1993) No agency is an island. *Security Management*, 37, pp 25-28.

21. Finan, I. (1994) NCIS offers partnership with local law enforcement. *The Police Chief*, 61 (September), pp 56-57.

22. van den Bergh, E. (1995) Crime prevention on industrial sites. *Security Journal*, in press.
    van Dijk, J. (1995) In search of synergy: coalition building against crime in The Netherlands. *Security Journal*, in press.

23. de Waard, J. (1995). Introduction to the 'Dutch Special'. *Security Journal*, in press.

24. Hesseling, R. (1995) Functional surveillance in The Netherlands. *Security Journal*, in press.

25. Klein, L., Luxenburg, J. and King, M. (1989) Perceived neighbourhood crime and the impact of private security. *Crime and Delinquency*, 35, pp 365-377.

26. Trajanowicz, R. and Bucqueroux, B. (1990) The privatisation of public justice: what will it mean for the police? *The Police Chief*, 57 (October), pp 131-135.

27. Shearing, C. and Brogden, M. (1993) *Policing for a New South Africa*. London: Routledge.

28. Doob, A. (ed) (1993) *Thinking about Police Resources*. Toronto: Centre of Criminology, University of Toronto.

Opportunities for Crime Prevention: The Need for Incentives

Ken Pease

Summary

- Prevention should be the single task of crime control.

- Crime prevention can be achieved by reducing opportunities to offend as well as by the detection and punishment of offenders.

- Preventive measures can substantially control certain types of crime and the fear that crime will simply be displaced elsewhere is no longer a valid excuse for not introducing such measures.

- Minor changes in administrative procedures by government departments could reduce opportunities for certain types of offence.

- The police, citizens, businesses and local authorities need incentives to introduce crime prevention measures.

- The extent to which introducing incentives for crime prevention infringe civil liberties needs to be debated.

Introduction

Crime increases as the opportunity to commit crime increases. As video recorders become lighter and more common, more are stolen because it is easier to do so. Crime will increase as the period between sexual maturity and economic independence lengthens and enlarges the pool of young people tempted and capable of committing crime. As people recognise fewer and fewer of the young living in their neighbourhood, crime will increase because community surveillance is diminished. In short, crime mirrors and measures changes in everyday life.[1] Without extensive action to offset the crime harvest of social changes, we can

96

expect continuing growth in crime, accelerated or slowed only by the current stage of the economic cycle.[2]

John Donne begged God not to make him the gateway to another man's sin. By offering a plethora of criminal opportunities to those whom we go on to punish, we are doing just that. I shall argue that effective crime prevention is possible, what is missing is a system of incentives to encourage the public, local authorities, industry and commerce and the police to make it a reality.

The effectiveness of crime prevention

The belief that preventing one form of crime will result in increases in another, or that preventing crime in one area will result in its displacement to another, has long been a tapeworm in the gut of crime prevention policy, sapping its vitality and justifying inaction. But the research literature is consistent in showing that major reductions in certain types of crime can be achieved.[3] Improving the security of new and used cars in West Germany reduced vehicle crime, concerted action by the alcohol and tobacco industries reduced thefts of goods in transit, to name but two of the many successes achieved. Where crime reduction does occur, typically only a small proportion of prevented crime is displaced elsewhere.[4] Reduction of car theft in West Germany was not accompanied by an increase in the theft of motor cycles, reduction of burglaries in Rochdale was not associated with an increase in acquisitive crimes in adjacent areas. There may well be particular crime types where *all* prevented crime is displaced to another time or place – cross-national drug trafficking is a contender for total displacement. This, however, is very much the exception.

When a crime prevention initiative is mooted, there will always be someone who doubts its worth on the grounds that crime will be displaced elsewhere. Strangely, few argue that preventing crime in a restricted area will also prevent crime in surrounding areas, with offenders being unaware of the precise limits of the prevention efforts. Yet this bonus, known as the diffusion of benefits, is as likely to occur as displacement. Crime prevention effects do 'leak' to adjacent areas or to crimes which were not targeted by the preventive action. Instances of this have been found in crimes as diverse as burglary prevention and fare evasion.[5]

While some crimes have yielded more easily to situational measures than others, the limits on situational prevention have not been reached.

Opportunities for violent crime may be restricted by the sale of drinks in plastic glasses in sports stadia and by the use in pubs of safety glasses which do not shatter on impact. Providing quick response alarms to women who have been the victims of violence at the hands of former partners is another example.

Besides the obvious benefits of reduced crime, crime prevention efforts have other attractions, not least in delaying and disrupting the development of individual criminal careers. This occurs both directly, by making recruitment to crime and criminal apprenticeships more hazardous, and indirectly, by freeing police resources to deal with more serious crime. Since the longest and most serious criminal careers also tend to be the most diverse,[6] the two effects interact helpfully.

Thus, the problem is not the absence of effective crime prevention measures. Rather it is that the use of the repertoire of techniques for crime prevention has been limited by their perceived marginality to the central aims of policing despite the lip service paid to it by central Government and the police themselves. The absence of incentives for the citizen to prevent crime lies at the heart of the problem.

Administrative procedures and crime prevention

Two examples of administrative procedures suffice to illustrate the failure to implement simple crime prevention measures that would save the resources of the police as well as those of the rest of the criminal justice system.

The first example relates to car theft where the current procedures of the Department of Transport and the behaviour of car insurers make car 'ringing' much easier than it need be. About a third of stolen cars are not recovered, either being dismantled for parts or 'rung'. Two cars are involved in the ringing process: the body donor is the stolen car and the identity donor is usually a car that has been 'written-off' as irreparably damaged by an insurance company. Although there is a voluntary process whereby such write-offs are notified to the Driver and Vehicle Licensing Agency (DVLA) by the insurance companies, notification often does not happen. In any case, owners of written-off cars which were only insured against third-party risks keep their title to the car and can sell directly to ringers. The written-off car can be sold and bought through the motor trade papers where advertisements include coded phrases like 'not recorded', while others specifically offer to buy third-party write-offs. Legally valid tax disks can be obtained by pretending to have lost the ownership documents and by completing the appropriate application form. Professional thieves will do this for a job lot of stolen cars in one transaction using a single stolen cheque and a false address. The cheque bounces but a set of stolen cars will have valid tax disks.

There are many administrative solutions to car 'ringing'. For example, where the registration document is not presented when a car is taxed, a distinctively coloured tax disk could be issued limited to one month validity, with the six or twelve month disk sent to the address supplied in the tax application. This arrangement would make ringing more difficult and far less attractive.

The second example involves credit card fraud. Until recently the procedures of credit card companies, in sending cards by ordinary post without a separate activation procedure, resulted in high fraudulent losses. Taking elementary precautions (such as the requirement to collect the card from a bank or building society) reduced fraudulent losses by a fifth in the first year after they were introduced.[7] In Sweden issuing cheque guarantee and credit cards bearing the owner's photograph reduced cheque forgeries to 10 per cent of their previous level.[8]

Advantages of crime prevention measures to the citizen

Economically rational people will protect themselves against crime risk 'until an additional pound spent on crime prevention will yield less than a pound's worth of prevented crime'.[9] Of course, this point comes more swiftly when crime costs are borne by an insurer. In this sense, insurance serves to reduce the level of crime prevention precautions taken by individuals.

Householders' crime prevention efforts benefit themselves and society as a whole by keeping down household insurance premiums, by increasing the value of property in the neighbourhood because of the lower risk of burglary, by reducing the costs of police time in investigating burglaries as well as the costs to the criminal justice system of dealing with apprehended burglars.

It has been argued that, with the co-operation of the insurance industry, governments could promote self-protection against crime by individuals, companies and services, as well as providing subsidies for security improvements. The European Union could insist on the adoption of a set of security standards in its member states.[10]

Incentives for crime prevention

Effective crime prevention does not require an elaborate set of new techniques but a system of incentives for individuals, the police and society at large, to ensure that security measures that are viable and socially advantageous are installed.

Local authorities could play a more active part in some forms of crime prevention if the incentive of extra funds from the Rate Support Grant paid by central government were to be made contingent upon reductions in calls for police service for criminal incidents in the area. In these circumstances an economically rational local authority would seek out those crimes which present particular problems. For example, because there is good evidence that burgled dwellings are at high risk of revictimisation during the six weeks that follow the first offence,[11] security in recently burgled council dwellings would be up-rated, with subsidies offered to residents in other types of property to do the same. Up-rated domestic security measures should go beyond the tokenism of installing window locking devices. Car parks from which cars are frequently stolen could be identified and the owners encouraged to install manned payment booths. Residents in council property causing misery to their neighbours could be evicted. Security in schools could be increased – burglars frequently use the same door or window which is usually (albeit tardily) replaced with no additional security precautions.

The business rate for factories, companies and shops could be used to encourage them to increase their precautions against crime by adjusting it according to their calls for police service, with those calling the police most frequently paying a higher rate. Alternatively, (and without overtones of victim-blaming) the business rate could be discounted for those who take agreed security measures. Shops could be encouraged to make shoplifting less easy by changing their layouts – research in two shopping malls found that some 80 per cent of calls for the police came from 20 per cent of the shops.[12]

Adjustments to the business rate might not be trivial for a large company and risk local employment loss if the company moved away as a result. Another option might be the involvement of the Health and Safety Executive (or some equivalent agency) at the invitation of the police, perhaps after three calls for police service within three months. If the HSE inspector found the company's security arrangements were not commensurate with the value of goods or equipment held, or the safety from crime of employees, enforcement notices could be issued to up-rate security to an appropriate level.

Other incentives to enhance security measures might include the publication by the police of the victimisation records of local factories, companies and businesses to bring pressure to bear on them. In the United States this is done for some shopping malls, and universities are required to inform the Congress of levels of crime victimisation on their campuses.[13]

The National Audit Commission could investigate the extent to which the procedures of Government departments and agencies contribute to crime (see example above of the DVLA). This would include systems of dispensing social security benefits and detection of tax fraud.

The role of the police

Crime prevention is not a glamorous part of police work. At the heart of police activity has lain the division between crime prevention and detection. This is an artificial distinction, which I would prefer to replace by the single aim of crime prevention, which may be achieved by detecting offenders or deflecting them from desirable targets by removing easy opportunities. Currently, operational detectives do not consider crime prevention as having anything to do with them, except as seeing such work as a pleasant pre-retirement posting for detectives who have exhausted themselves in the police service. Force organisation over the last fifteen years has reinforced the spurious distinction between detection and prevention by locating responsibility for crime prevention in the Community Affairs Department rather than as part of the Criminal Investigation Department. The status of crime prevention, in consequence, remains low and its funding trivial by contrast to that of other criminal justice functions. Less than 1 per cent of expenditure on criminal justice goes towards crime prevention. Less than a million pounds was spent in 1991/92 on the Home Office Crime Prevention Centre[14], where police officers and others are trained in prevention techniques, and which is housed in a glorified Portakabin behind Staffordshire Police Headquarters.

There is a lack of awareness by the police either that successful crime control is possible, or an awareness that it is not taken to be central to the evaluation of their work. For example, a study of the work of police officers responsible for crime prevention found that areas with the most crime were also areas with fewest officers with a responsibility for crime prevention.[15] This was true both within and between force areas. Crime prevention work was resourced as a marginal, if worthy, use of police time when the real work of responding to crime allowed. An as yet unpublished study by the present writer and colleagues on fast reductions in rates of recorded crime found that forces were typically unaware of where and when such declines occurred in their area.

It has been demonstrated that the logic of crime prevention is extremely simple, as are its implications for police work. The role of the police would continue to be the recording of criminal incidents and the prevention of their repetition through the detection of offenders. Their involvement in reducing the opportunities to offend (i.e. prevention by deflection) would cease to be one of exhortation and persuasion but more to identify the locations where crime most frequently occurs. For example, instead of begging a local authority or business to improve the security of its car parks, the police would pass the information to whatever agency was empowered and motivated to take crime prevention action. A business or local authority given a vested interest in crime reduction would need little persuasion to co-operate. Admittedly, many police forces would have to improve their information systems in order to identify crime patterns in ways that suggest prevention strategies. Already crime pattern analysis is used by some forces, and the use of incentives, for example, the provision of extra funds for police pay in areas where effective crime prevention measures are introduced could hasten crime pattern analysis development and use.

The infringement of civil liberties is the most frequently encountered objection to increasing incentives for crime prevention measures as proposed here. It can be argued that individuals, businesses and other organisations should be free to conduct themselves in grossly criminogenic ways whatever the cost to themselves and the rest of society. The civil liberties argument must be confronted and debated if we are serious about wanting to reduce the extent of crime. But for many categories of public well-being there are enforceable obligations not to damage the quality of life, for example, by environmental pollution. Why should crime be the exception?

Civil liberties apart, the greatest practical problem in providing incentives for crime prevention is that it would be difficult to do piecemeal. What is needed is a demonstration project by a police force covering one local authority area which could be offered bonuses from the Rate Support Grant for crime reductions during, say, a trial period of two years.

Conclusions

Research on crime prevention leads me to the following conclusions:

(a) most of the major social determinants of crime are outside the control of the police service, but

(b) by reducing opportunities to offend crime prevention is demonstrably possible, yet

(c) the police have not organised themselves as though crime prevention was a central objective of their work, while

(d) a system of incentives to encourage the implementation of a variety of crime prevention measures by individuals, companies, local authorities and government departments could reduce levels of crime considerably.

It is only possible to separate crime prevention and crime detection when sight of the principal purpose of the police has been lost. What is crime detection for? Any answer not restricted to vengeance against the offender must take crime prevention as its justification. Crime prevention should be the single supra-ordinate aim of policing. Effective crime prevention measures would reduce the costs of policing, and of the rest of the criminal justice system, as well as reducing the financial and emotional costs to the victims.

References

1. Felson, M. (1994) *Crime and Everyday Life*. London: Pine Forge Press.

2. Field, S. (1989) *Trends in Crime and Their Interpretation: A Study of Recorded Crime in Post-war England and Wales*. Home Office Research Study No. 119. London: HMSO.

3. Clarke, R.V.G. (ed) (1992, 1993, 1994) *Crime Prevention Studies*. Volumes 1, 2, 3. Monsey NY: Criminal Justice Press.

4. Barr, R. and Pease, K. (1990) Crime placement, displacement and deflection. In Tonry, M. and Morris, N. (eds) *Crime and Justice: an Annual Review of Research*. Volume 12. Chicago: University of Chicago Press.

5. Clarke, R.V.G. and Weisburd, D. (1994) Diffusion of crime control benefits: observations on the reverse of displacement. In Clarke, R.V.G. (ed) *Crime Prevention Studies*. Volume 2. Monsey NY: Criminal Justice Press.

6. Blumstein, A. et al. (1986) *Criminal Careers and Career Criminals*. (2 volumes). Washington DC: National Academy Press.

7. British Retail Consortium (1995) *Alert Issue 5*. London: Paragon Communications.

8. Knutsson, J. and Kuhlhorn, E. (1992) Macro-measures against crime: the case of check forgeries. In Clarke, R.V.G. (ed) *Situational Crime Prevention: Successful Case Studies*. New York: Harrow and Heston.

9. Field, S. and Hope, T. (1989) Economics, the consumer, and the under-provision of crime prevention. *Paper presented to the British Criminology Conference.*

10. van Dijk, J.J.M. (1994) Understanding crime rates. *British Journal of Criminology*, 34, pp 105-121.

11. Farrell, G. and Pease, K. (1993) *Once Bitten, Twice Bitten.* Crime Prevention Paper No. 46. London: Home Office.

12. Buck, W. (1994) *Evaluating a shopwatch scheme in Merseyside Police C division.* University of Manchester: M.A Econ. thesis.

13. Hope, T.J. Personal communication.

14. Barclay, G.C. (ed) (1993) *Digest 2: Information on the Criminal Justice System in England and Wales.* London: Home Office Research and Statistics Department.

15. Harvey, L., Grimshaw, P. and Pease, K. (1989) Crime prevention delivery: the work of police crime prevention officers. In Morgan, R. and Smith, D.J. (eds) *Coming to Terms with Policing.* London: Routledge.

The Regulation and Control of the Private Security Industry

Trevor Jones and *Tim Newburn*

Summary

- The significant growth of private security in recent years together with the expansion in the range of tasks it undertakes, has focused attention on the need for regulation and control of the industry.

- Currently, there is no formal statutory system of licensing of private security personnel in Britain. This is in direct contrast to almost every other Western European nation.

- The major issues which underlie calls for regulation concern low pay, levels of training in the industry, reliability of private security personnel, standards of service, and the protection of privacy.

- Models of regulation that could be adopted include voluntary or statutory self-regulation, or statutory public regulation. The latter could take one of several forms: central government control, local authority control.

Introduction

The growth of the private security industry, not only in terms of absolute size but also in the range of the 'policing' tasks it undertakes, raise questions about the need for regulation and control.

It is important to clarify what is, or might be, included under the rubric 'private security industry'. The bi-annual survey of the industry by Jordan and Sons defines it as 'concerned with the protection of physical property, assets and individuals from theft or violence' and distinguishes between firms which install physical/mechanical devices, or electrical/electronic surveillance apparatus, or provide staffed services.[1] However, this definition covers only those organisations and individuals who sell their products or services, and excludes the large 'in-house' security sector and private investigators as well as the many specialist 'security consultants' whose activities range across all three categories.

The difficulties in providing a clear definition of the industry are partly due to its blurred edges as a result of diversification. Large firms like Securicor, for example, have moved in to the development and application of mobile communication systems. An increasing number of office maintenance and cleaning firms are undertaking security functions as well as their core business, perhaps offering a complete package deal of expertise in alarm systems and security-vetted staff. Thus, 'on a continuum of a whole range of commercial services, it is now increasingly difficult to say where the private security sector begins or ends'.[2]

When considering possible means of regulating this industry it is vital to recognise that however the private security sector is defined, it encompasses a wide range of firms undertaking a variety of activities. Consequently, what may be an appropriate model for regulating one part of the industry may be entirely inappropriate for another.

The need for regulation

The private security sector in the UK is not entirely unregulated by statute. There are some areas where general legal rules apply, for example, the regulations relating to the carrying of firearms. There are also some more specific provisions in statutes: the Police Act 1964 s52(1) made it an offence for private security guards to wear uniforms intended to mislead the public into believing they are police officers, and the 1975 Guard Dogs Act regulates the use of such dogs.

The issue of how to improve regulation of the industry has been raised in public debate repeatedly since the 1970s. For some time the Government has supported the voluntary self-regulation approach. For example, in 1983 the then Home Secretary, Douglas Hurd, said 'It remains our view that the case for statutory control of the industry has not been made out. As you know, the Government has instead encouraged self-regulation by the industry'. Thus, no licensing system, or other formal system of Government regulation, has been introduced except in Northern Ireland where, under the Northern Ireland (Emergency Provisions) Act 1987, a system of public licensing of private security personnel has been operation since 1988. In this respect, Britain contrasts with most other European countries. Austria, Belgium, Denmark, Finland, France, Germany, Greece, Italy, Netherlands, Norway, Portugal, Spain, Sweden and Switzerland all have some form of legislative control of their private security industry.[3]

Recent years have seen growing demands for the introduction of statutory controls mainly because of concerns about low pay, rectitude, standards of service and privacy. Such demands have come from the Labour Party, trades unions, the police service, and latterly, the main trade associations operating within the industry. The first report of the enquiry into the industry by the Home Affairs Select Committee recommended only that the contract guarding sector should be subject to statutory licensing.[4] This recommendation was widely welcomed, and the Home Secretary is currently considering his response.

Growth of the industry

Although a range of estimates of employment and turnover exist, there is general consensus that the industry has undergone a striking expansion over recent years.[5] Along with the growth in absolute size the industry has been taking on new tasks and responsibilities, including the operation of private prisons and prisoner escort services, and security firms are increasingly undertaking tasks which were previously seen as the preserve of the public police. Perhaps the most publicised example of the latter is the employment of private uniformed patrols on residential estates.[6]

In 1993 the establishment of a Home Office Review of Police Core and Ancillary Tasks was seen in some quarters as the prelude to a programme of contracting-out further police tasks to the private sector. The findings of the Review should, however, have at least temporarily allayed these fears, for it only identified a limited number of tasks as suitable for hiving-off.[7]

Low pay

It has been argued that low pay and poor conditions of employment in the private security industry were encouraged by the economic conditions during the early 1980s and 1990s. The recession failed to diminish the demand for private security, with empty warehouses and offices needing guarding, while surviving companies were unable to bear the costs of crime.[8]

Several surveys have shown that low pay and poor working conditions characterise guarding services (static and mobile guarding, cash-in-transit etc.) which are closely related to the market structure of this part of the industry. There are relatively few 'barriers to entry' to this sector which contains many small firms engaging in fierce competition so that the incentive to reduce labour costs to a minimum is high.

A survey in 1983 of firms providing guarding services found that a high proportion paid low basic wages, and employees had to rely on overtime and shift work to make up their take-home pay to reasonable levels.[9] The report commented that 'shift working is a way of life for the security industry ... yet there is very little recognition of this in the pay packet ... very many companies simply have no shift premium at all'. It is important to note that the findings from this survey were based on responses from unionised workplaces only. Wages and working conditions are likely to be considerably poorer in the larger non-unionised sector. In 1984 a researcher commented 'in the unorganised sector of private security, pay and conditions fall well below recognised standards and are among the worst in any industry today'.[10] Another used New Earnings Survey data to argue that on two definitions of 'low pay', and when weekly earnings exclude the effects of overtime, over a quarter of all security guards and officers were low paid, compared to about 18 per cent of all male workers.[11] More recently, a survey in 1993 found hourly pay rates for contract guarding ranging from £1.79 to £4.35, with over a third in a band between £2.30 and £2.60.[12]

The Trades Union Congress, examining arguments for a statutory minimum wage, found that contract guarding is one of a number of sectors which have been increasingly characterised by low pay and poor working conditions.[13] A number of trades unions have been campaigning for a minimum wage of £4.15 an hour. Given the hourly wage rates currently found to be common for contract guarding this level would have extremely important implications for this sector independently of any system of regulation which may be introduced.

Training

Inadequate levels of training have been raised as a central problem of the private security industry by a number of commentators.[14] High levels of unemployment provide a large pool of labour for security companies to choose from and, with high staff turnover, largely caused by the poor wages, there is no incentive for most smaller employers to provide anything other than minimal training. Further, there is a lack of higher education training in security matters in the UK compared with the United States.

Some of the industry associations, notably the International Professional Security Association (IPSA), have developed training courses and conferences, and large companies have developed quite extensive training facilities – Group 4 and Securicor have their own training schools. The prospects for training in the industry were improved with the establishment of the Security Industry Training Organisation (SITO) in 1991. SITO was recognised by the (then) Department for Education as the official training body of the industry, and has developed National Vocational Qualifications (NCVQ), which involve a comprehensive framework of occupational standards. SITO has two national training centres, and a further seven centres at the regional level.[15]

Rectitude

A strong theme running through police criticisms of the private security industry is the unreliability of staff. Given the low levels of pay in the staffed sector, easy access to property and cash could be a source of temptation. In 1988 a report by the Association of Chief Police Officers (ACPO) highlighted a number of deficiencies in the industry, particularly 'employer/employee having a criminal record'.[16] In its evidence to the Home Affairs Committee in 1994, ACPO again suggested that there was a high incidence of criminal records amongst employees of private security firms.[17]

It has been argued that the trade associations accept the existence of criminal infiltration, but pass this off with the 'rotten apples' argument, in order to enhance the public image of the industry.[2] The fact that private security companies are not exempt from the provisions of the Rehabilitation of Offenders Act 1974 means that there are difficulties for companies that wish to vet staff. The trade associations have long argued that companies should be exempted, and this is supported by the pro-regulation lobby.

Some sources within the industry[18] have argued that there is nothing inherent in private security work which attracts people with criminal records:

> The problem is not that the industry is full of criminals. It is that it has more than its fair share of the disadvantaged and disaffected for whom the low pay and long hours make security work a last resort option...

There are no comparative data about criminal involvement for other service industries operating in similar labour markets, such as contract cleaning or hotels and catering. However, it is reasonable to argue that these sectors, too, are likely to have more than their fair share of people who have been convicted of criminal offences. From this viewpoint, the occupational comparisons of offending rates which ACPO presented in evidence to the Home Affairs Committee were perhaps not as surprising as they might at first seem. In the Lancashire force area during 1993-94, the offending rates per 1000 employees in the private security industry, post office and police service were 29, 12 and 2 respectively. It would be interesting to have similar figures for other industries relying on trust but operating in the same peripheral labour market.[19] Employees of contract cleaning companies, for example, are often low-paid, poorly-qualified, work unsocial hours and have extensive access to private property.

Standards of service

It has been argued that a poor standard of product is a problem which applies particularly to the intruder alarm sector, despite the application of British Standards for some years, with 'enormous' numbers of public complaints about faulty alarm systems.[20] It is certainly the case that the vast majority of system activations are false alarms. This has, over the years, been a huge drain on police resources and led in 1990 to the introduction of a national burglar alarm policy by ACPO involving withdrawal of response to frequently activated devices. The number of false activations reported in the 1990 National Intruder Alarm Statistics published by ACPO showed a 3 per cent decline on the previous year although the proportion of false alarms remained very high. Even so, the Home Affairs Committee considered that the systems installation sector was not at present a suitable case for the introduction of statutory controls.

The highly competitive nature of the industry has been related to problems with product quality such as corner-cutting and sharp practice.[2] Examples of sharp practice include guards who are supposed to be keeping an all night watch turning up only last thing at night and first thing in the morning. The high incidence of casual, seasonal or previously unemployed labour in the guarding sector may increase this tendency for sharp practice and lowers costs for the firms. However, there is only limited anecdotal evidence to support allegations of widespread malpractice.

The 'cut-throat' nature of the market in contract security is often seen as the culprit for such behaviour. In evidence to the Home Affairs Committee, Securicor highlighted the problem of consumers of contract security making decisions based only on overall cost and not considering the issue of quality. This was, in their opinion, because the employment of contract guarding services was usually a 'grudge purchase', done for the sake of appearance rather than due to any significant perceived benefit.[4]

A number of other problems, including shady activities of some firms operating in the personal protection or body-guarding market, have been raised including the possibility that professional bodyguards or minders may well carry arms illegally.[2] Again, there is little evidence as to the extent of such problems although there is concern about activities which frequently involve personal violence. The problem of 'strong-arm' tactics is most usually associated with night club door supervisors, with a number of highly-publicised incidents of assaults on customers. Some police forces and local authorities (for example, the London boroughs of Westminster and Wandsworth) have introduced voluntary registration schemes for door-supervisors. Another area which is sometimes associated with excessive violence is the bailiffing market. Some security firms advertise one of their services as the eviction of squatters and there are reports of criminal assaults by their staff when carrying out such tasks.[2]

Privacy

Another major area of concern is intrusion on privacy, and this particularly relates to the private investigation sector. As long ago as 1972 the Younger Committee recommended that this sector should be subject to statutory regulation.[21] Again, detailed evidence about malpractice is, not surprisingly, thin on the ground, but there have been reports that private investigators have broken the law to satisfy clients by 'bugging' premises, committing criminal damage or even burglary.[22] There have been major developments in electronic surveillance and tapping equipment over recent years[23] with a resultant expansion in the potential for abuse of privacy. The 1993/4 IPSA yearbook includes an article entitled 'Stopping the rot of disloyalty' which claims that 'every company large enough to employ people is under attack from within', citing a range of misdemeanours from fiddling expense claims to deliberate conspiracy to steal company secrets. To counter this, companies can go to firms which supply a range of products 'from the basic inexpensive bug, to highly sophisticated devices such as briefcases, pens and calculators containing high security UHF radio microphones'.

Models of regulation

Given the range of problems associated with the private security industry, along with its significant growth both in terms of size and function over recent years, there now appears to be a broad consensus in support of some form of statutory regulation. However, important questions remain about how such regulation should be organised and administered.

Conservative governments have been particularly reluctant to introduce statutory regulation on the grounds that in a free market the optimal outcome is reached by allowing the market to regulate itself, with competition ensuring that companies which provide a poor standard of product, or habitually employ poorly-trained or untrustworthy people, will go out of business as customers turn to alternative suppliers. This, of course, is based on the false assumption that consumers have access to complete information within the market. The Government's view so far has been that the industry should be allowed to regulate itself, and that calls from larger companies for public licensing are based on a desire to eliminate the competition from smaller firms who provide a cheaper service.

Voluntary self-regulation

The main criticism of the existing system of self-regulation is that it is voluntary: only the minority of firms in the industry who choose to join one of the trade/professional associations are subject to any regulation at all. Furthermore, doubts have been raised about how strictly standards are enforced amongst the relatively few firms who do submit to voluntary regulation.

The most influential voluntary regulatory body is the British Security Industry Association (BSIA). Some 240 firms, with a total annual turnover of £1.7billion which employ 74,000 staff involved in security activities, are members. Although the membership remains small in terms of total numbers of firms, it includes some of the largest and most influential companies. For many years the BSIA publically opposed statutory regulation of the industry but has recently reversed this position.

Since the 1970s the BSIA has developed standards, codes of practice and other initiatives to regulate the conduct of member companies. Its attempts to regulate the intruder alarm sector led to the establishment of a National Supervisory Council for Intruder Alarms (NSCIA) which in 1991 merged with another inspecting body, the Security Systems

Inspectorate (SSI), to become the National Approval Council for Security Systems (NACOSS).

The Manned Services Inspectorate (MSI) was formed by the BSIA in 1982 as a quality control body for the manned (sic) sector. In 1992, the MSI was merged into a new 'independent' inspectorate, set up jointly by the BSIA and the International Professional Security Association (IPSA). This new Inspectorate for the Security Industry (ISI) included representatives of the industry, insurers, customers, the police and government departments. The ISI inspects guarding and cash-in-transit companies against British Standard BS 7499 and industry codes of practice. This joint venture led to speculation that the two main associations in the private security industry were considering a merger but this diminished when IPSA withdrew from the ISI.

A number of doubts have been raised as to the effectiveness of these self-regulatory bodies, for example, there is no record of any member company being expelled for disciplinary reasons.[24] Although BSIA standards include employment checks, the codes allow provisional employment for commercial reasons. Perhaps more importantly, all inspection visits to companies are pre-arranged. As the Home Affairs Committee heard, there are doubts about how far these inspectorates are independent of the security industry and it has been suggested that 'the ethos of ISI is part of the ethos of the big security companies'.[25]

IPSA represents both organisations and individuals concerned with security, membership being open to all employers of, or employees engaged in, private security work on a full-time basis. IPSA have been active in developing training standards and arranging courses and conferences. It founded the International Institute of Security which requires membership of IPSA for a year before joining and passing an examination covering a wide range of security matters. The Institute also offers a number of correspondence training courses.

In March 1990 IPSA established the British Security Register of the personal details and employment histories of individuals working within the industry. The primary function of this Register is to provide employers with a reliable source of reference but also to improve the credibility of those who are registered. However, the voluntary nature of Register makes it inevitable that it includes only a fraction of those working in the industry.

There are a number of other specialist representative organisations. The main body representing the lockmaking industry is the Master Locksmith's Association (MLA). Along with many other bodies in this sector, MLA have tended to favour a system of licensing or regulation, mainly due to the fear of expanded (and perhaps unscrupulous) competition. There has been a massive expansion in the number of lock-cutting and fitting outlets, for example, in 'heel-bars'. There are fears that the quality of product will be reduced, as well as concerns that certain suppliers may use their skills to gain access to properties for criminal purposes.

The Home Affairs Committee concluded that 'the case has not been made out for statutory regulation of the systems installation sector of the industry and that voluntary regulation has established itself as an effective force in this field'.[4] There are two main bodies currently involved in the certification and approval of security systems, NACOSS (see above) and the smaller Security Systems and Alarms Inspections Board (SSAIB). In evidence to the Home Affairs Committee NACOSS claimed that companies registered with it were responsible for over 90 per cent of installations in the commercial market during 1994. This high degree of market penetration has been attributed to insurance companies laying down requirements for equipment before agreeing to provide cover, and also to police forces requiring that registered installers are used before accepting the installations which activate alarm signals at a police station. This, in itself, might be taken to illustrate the importance of a degree of compulsion in the regulation process.

The private investigation sector has two main representative bodies. The major industry body is the Association of British Investigators (ABI). This organisation has openly criticised the standards of conduct of some parts of the sector, and lays emphasis on its code of ethics, and the use of its membership list by the Law Society. In the past it has leaned towards a system of control or licensing for private investigators, as witnessed by its submission to the 1979 Royal Commission on Legal Services.[2] There is also a professional association, the Institute of Professional Investigators (IPI). This requires members to hold either a vocational qualification at management level or an academic qualification of 'appropriate standing'.[26] The IPI remains strongly in favour of formal regulation of the sector, and was critical of the Home Affairs Committee's concentration on the contract guarding side of the security industry.[27]

Statutory self-regulation

Statutory self-regulation could involve regulation via the existing industry inspectorates. As this would be the least costly option of any of the suggested forms of improved regulation, it is perhaps the most likely to find favour with the Government. This model is supported by the BSIA which, in its submission to the Home Affairs Committee, suggested that the staffed sector should be subject to statutory controls, and that 'the ISI, either as a contractor to, or part of, a statutory licensing body, could provide cost effective inspection and accreditation services'.[28] One criticism of this mode of regulation is that the regulatory bodies would be dominated by the major interests within the industry, and would thus lack independence. In addition, there would be the difficulty of deciding which organisation would carry out the regulatory functions, particularly in the light of the recent distancing of IPSA from BSIA.

Statutory public regulation

This would involve statutory licensing with regulation to be carried out by an independent inspectorate. It is the approach favoured by Bruce George MP, who has introduced a number of Private Member's Bills in unsuccessful attempts to bring about public regulation of the industry. A number of models have been considered.

Self-regulation with public participation

This would be similar to the system of regulation in the advertising industry. The Advertising Standards Authority (ASA) was established in 1972 and since 1974 has been funded by the imposition of a 0.1 per cent surcharge on the cost of advertisements (other than classified advertisements). There are a host of statutory restrictions intended to restrain the publication of misleading or indecent advertisements which are supplemented by the voluntarily accepted codes of conduct drawn up by the ASA. The ASA has a chairperson who must be independent of the advertising industry, as must the majority of the members of its Council. The chairperson appoints the members of the board. The codes of practice are drawn up by a committee representing interests from the advertising industry which consults closely with the ASA and with consumer groups. The codes are enforced by an ASA recommendation that offenders be denied advertising space or trading privileges, or by the ASA publicizing cases of companies who have contravened the codes. The ASA advertises itself as a body to whom complaints can be submitted. Despite this, the ASA is criticised as having too few sanctions to be an effective regulator of the advertising industry.

Central government control

In 1984 Bruce George suggested a particular aspect of the work of the Office of Fair Trading (OFT) could, in theory, be applied to the private security industry.[14] This relates to the licensing by OFT of businesses concerned with the granting of credit, the hiring of goods, and other ancillary credit activities. The criteria laid out by the Fair Trading Act 1973 for the granting of licences would be readily applicable to the security industry, particularly those on the criminal record of the applicant, and engaging in 'deceitful or oppressive' business practices. Direct controls such as these would avoid the need to create a new tier in the regulatory structure, would be cheaper, and direct control by civil servants would avoid conflicts of interest. However, the disadvantages include remoteness from the industry, lack of necessary experience, and inflexibility.

Public licensing

The model which Bruce George has repeatedly argued for – and he is the longest-standing advocate of regulation – is one of public licensing. This would avoid the inflexibility of direct government regulation, but could not be evaded as with self-regulation. The model he has proposed is set out in his 1994 Private Member's Bill 'Private Security (Registration) Bill' and applies to all sectors of the industry. It required the establishment of a national independent authority to licence and register firms and employees, with an inspectorate employed to enforce regulations under the control of the independent authority. Such regulation would ensure minimum requirements for companies and employees, for example, firms would need to be properly insured, provide appropriate training, and offer acceptable employment conditions. There would also be checks on the character and experience of management and employees, with codes of conduct for the different sectors of the industry.

Local authority control

Another possible model is regulation by local authorities, who already undertake a variety of regulatory functions in matters such as environmental health, planning, trading standards, and entertainments licensing. Some local authorities have already become involved in regulating one part of the security sector, night club door staff, by requiring anyone wishing to work as a door supervisor at a club in the area to register with them. Registration usually requires the applicant undergoing some basic training as well as being passed as 'suitable' by the local police, with the granting of entertainment licences to premises being conditional on the employment of registered door staff.

Critics of this model argue that local authorities and the police are already overwhelmed with regulatory functions, and lack the necessary experience of the security industry. Against this, however, the industry contains many small firms operating in a highly localised area. This may suggest that registration could more effectively be undertaken by local authorities. However, both they and the police are unlikely to be willing to take on the major task of licensing all parts of the security industry given the current constraints on their resources.

Conclusions

The growing significance of the private security industry has focused attention on the lack of provision for regulation and control. In 1995 the main recommendation in the first report of the Home Affairs Committee on the industry was limited to the establishment of a public licensing system of both companies and individuals in the contract guarding sector.[4] This would involve the formation of a self-financing agency with a duty to screen and license individual guards and companies. The agency would be given access to criminal records. The report did not go into details about the structure of this new agency, other than broad recommendations that 'it must be clearly accountable to Parliament through the Home Secretary, that it should have strong links with the police and with industry and commerce, but that it must be independent of the security industry'. The report left the exact details for future consideration, but suggested that the agency should outline some minimum standards for training, pay and working conditions.

It is important to emphasise that detailed consideration needs to be given to the practicalities of the various options for public regulation of *all* the various sectors of the private security industry. As the Home Affairs Committee found, there is a lack of reliable information about the industry. Nevertheless, the growing demands for regulation will probably result in some action from the Home Secretary, whose support for voluntary self-regulation may have been terminally weakened by the change of heart of the BSIA. However, the government's free-market philosophy sits uneasily with state regulation, this together with its overarching concern with cost savings, and reluctance to increase local authority powers, suggests that the model of regulation selected will be based on the existing industry inspectorates. It remains to be seen whether this will be the option chosen, and if so, how effective it will prove to be.

References

1. Jordan and Sons Ltd. (1987, 1989, 1993) *Britain's Security Industry*. London: Jordan and Sons Ltd.

2. South, N. (1988) *Policing for Profit*. London: Sage.

3. de Waard, J. (1993) The private security sector in fifteen European countries: size, rules and legislation. *Security Journal*, 4, pp 58-63.

4. House of Commons Home Affairs Select Committee (1995) *The Private Security Industry*. First Report, Session 1994-95. London: HMSO.

5. Jones, T. and Newburn, T. (1995) How big is the private security sector? *Policing and Society*, 5, pp 221-232.

6. Fogg, E. and Brace, M. (1994) Private policing cuts crime on Islington estates. *The Independent*, August 16.

7. Home Office (1995) *Review of Police Core and Ancillary Tasks. Final Report*. London: HMSO.

8. Johnston, L. (1991) *The Rebirth of Private Policing*. London: Routledge.

9. MATSA (1983) *Report on the Private Security Industry*. Esher.

10. Williams, D., George, B. and MacLennan, E. (eds) (1984) *Guarding Against Low Pay*. Low Pay Unit.

11. Williams, D. (1984) The economics of security guarding. In Williams *et al. Guarding Against Low Pay*. London; Low Pay Unit.

12. West Midlands Low Pay Unit (1994) *Securing a Living Wage: A Study of the Pay and Conditions of Contract Security Guards*. Briefing Paper.

13. Trades Union Congress (1995) *Arguments for a Minimum Wage*. London: TUC.

14. George, B. (1984) The case for public control. In Williams, D., George, B. and MacLennan, E. (eds) *Guarding Against Low Pay* London: Low Pay Unit.
    Williams, D., George, B. and MacLennan, E. (eds) (1984) *Guarding Against Low Pay*. Low Pay Unit.
    South, N. (1988) *Policing for Profit*. London: Sage.
    Johnston, L. (1991) *The Rebirth of Private Policing*. London: Routledge.

15. Business Round Table (1994) *The Growing Demand for Security: Opportunities for UK Suppliers*. London: Business Round Table Ltd.

16. Association of Chief Police Officers (1988) *A Review of the Private Security Industry*. London: ACPO.

17. Association of Chief Police Officers (1994) *Evidence to the House of Commons Select Committee on the private security industry*.

18. King, J. (1995) Regulation – when will it come? *Security Gazette*, August, p 42.
19. Jordan and Sons Ltd. (1993) *Britain's Security Industry*. London: Jordan and Sons Ltd.
20. George, B. and Watson, T. (1992) Regulation of the private security industry. *Public Money and Management*, 12, pp 55-57.
21. Younger, K. (1972) *Report of the Committee on Privacy*. London: HMSO.
22. George, B. and Button, M. (1994) *The need for regulation of the private security industry*. A submission to the House of Commons Home Affairs Select Committee on the private security industry.
23. Lyon, D. (1994) *The Electronic Eye: The Rise of Surveillance Society*. Cambridge: Polity Press.
24. Jordan and Sons Ltd. (1993) *Britain's Security Industry*. London: Jordan and Sons Ltd.
25. George, B. quoted by House of Commons Home Affairs Select Committee (1995) *The Private Security Industry*. First Report, Session 1994-95. London: HMSO.
26. Jones, P. (1992) The real professional investigator. In *Security 92/93. The Official Reference Book of IPSA*.
27. Institute of Professional Investigators (1995) *Response to The Report of the Home Affairs Select Committee on the Private Security Industry*. Glasgow: IPI.
28. British Security Industry Association (1994) *Evidence to the House of Commons Select Committee on the private security industry*.

Police Accountability

Tim Newburn and *Trevor Jones*

Summary

- In the past most emphasis was laid on the *political* accountability of the police, but attention has now shifted to *financial* and *managerial* forms, with 'contractual and managerial' accountability underlying the philosophy of the Police and Magistrates Court Act 1994.

- As well as political, managerial and financial controls, the activities of the police are subject to regulation under the criminal and civil legal codes, with an independent Police Complaints Authority to consider complaints levelled at individual police officers by members of the public.

- External control mechanisms will not be effective unless they are supported by the police service itself, in terms of the occupational culture, the internal disciplinary system and by managerial supervision.

Introduction

During the 1980s concern with accountability was central to much of the discussion about policing in Britain. 'Accountability' has been called a 'chameleon word' because it encompasses a range of meanings including 'answerability, responsiveness, openness, efficient estate management, not to mention participation and obedience to external laws'.[1] There is a fundamental distinction between *political accountability* in the sense of people elected to run society's affairs having an obligation to explain and justify their conduct in public; and *financial accountability* in the sense of audit and stewardship. Whereas the former notion is characterised by fundamental disagreements about objectives, the latter is often presented as 'a neutral and technical exercise'.[1]

The debate about police accountability divided those who sought to extend the influence of local elected representatives over policing policy, and those who wished to preserve the 'operational independence' of chief constables. At one end of the spectrum, 'accountability' was interpreted as direct *control* of policing policy by elected representatives.[2] At the other, forms of external influence over policing policy were presented as unacceptable partisan interference, a view best expressed in Lord Denning's famous judgement that chief constables were 'answerable to the law and to the law alone'. The notion of accountability to the law remains a strong and enduring one in police rhetoric. More recently the debate has shifted away from political forms of accountability, with a growing emphasis on 'managerial and contractual' modes.[3] The Police and Criminal Evidence Act 1984 provided a framework for increased regulation of police powers through the police disciplinary process. This in turn focuses on another aspect of accountability, the problem of making police officers answerable for the use of their powers in particular cases.

Clearly 'police accountability' is a general concept which is difficult to encapsulate. Perhaps the most helpful definition is Bayley's:[4]

> An accountable police force shall be taken to be one whose actions, severally and collectively, are congruent with the values of the community in which it works and responsive to the discrepancies when they are pointed out.

Why accountability?

The most significant reason why the police should be held accountable is that they have at their disposal a range of coercive powers over the freedoms of citizens which have much potential for abuse. It is important that the police explain and justify the exercise of such extensive powers. In the financial sense of audit and stewardship, the police service is responsible for the expenditure of a significant amount of public funds and should be held to account for its effective use. A related point is that policing is an important public service involving the allocation of limited resources in the face of unlimited demand. Accountability should provide the public with some influence over the priorities for the distribution of resources. Another important aspect of accountability is its link to organisational legitimacy and through this to effectiveness. It is argued that a police service that is seen to be accountable will earn a high degree of public trust and co-operation and will therefore be more effective.

External mechanisms of accountability

General policy decisions

It is only relatively recently that 'policing policy' has become a subject for debate. Up until about 15 years ago it was often suggested that the task of the police was to 'enforce the law without fear or favour', and that the pattern of policing was simply determined by the legal system and its constitutional framework.[5] During the 1980s critics of this narrow legalistic interpretation of police accountability argued that, while the police obviously have a duty to enforce the law, this does not impose any particular pattern of policing because policing resources are limited, whereas the opportunities for law enforcement are limitless. Consequently, decisions must be taken about priorities or 'policing policy'.[6]

The Police Act 1964 provides the basis for the external controls over the police service in England and Wales, although it has recently been amended by the Police and Magistrates' Courts Act 1994. The 1964 Act laid down what has become known as the 'tripartite structure' which divided responsibility for the framing, monitoring and financing of policing policy between the Home Secretary, chief constables and local police authorities. It created police authorities for each of the 41 provincial police forces, with a membership consisting of two thirds councillors and one third magistrates. In London, no local body was created to administer the Metropolitan Police, whose police authority was, and remains, the Home Secretary.

The police authorities had a duty under the Act to secure the maintenance of an 'adequate and efficient' force for their area. They were empowered to appoint a chief constable, his deputy and assistants subject to the approval of the Home Secretary, determine the establishment and the budget of the force, and require the chief constable to submit annually a report in writing on matters concerning the policing of the area.

The only statutory duty owed by the chief constable to his police authority was the submission of an annual report. The authority could also 'require' that he provide a written report on any matter related to policing of the area. Though potentially powerful, this provision provided little actual leverage, for chief constables could refuse to make such a report if they believed it would contain information 'which in the public interest ought not to be disclosed, or is not needed for the discharge of the functions of the police authority'. This form of accountability was described as an 'explanatory and co-operative' mode in contrast to the 'subordinate and obedient' mode advanced by those who supported control of policing policy by elected representatives.[7]

One of the major changes made by the 1964 Act was the enshrining in statute of chief constables' supreme responsibility for local policing, each force being 'under the direction and control' of its chief officer. The Act, however, did not clearly demarcate the responsibilities of the different parties within the tripartite structure. It became widely assumed that the chief constable was responsible for 'operational matters', which in practice was interpreted broadly as including issues of general policy as well as decisions in individual cases. However, there was no legal principle preventing police authorities from issuing directions on matters of general policy.

A well-documented theme in writings about police accountability since the 1964 Police Act has been the relative impotence of police authorities compared with chief constables. However, the most influential pillar of tripartite structure is arguably the Home Secretary. Many of the powers conferred on the police authority could only be exercised with the approval of the Home Secretary. In addition, the Home Secretary can require a police authority to retire its chief constable 'in the interests of efficiency', though this provision was never formally invoked. Home Office influence has increased in recent years with the issuing of circulars of policy guidelines, the strengthening of Her Majesty's Inspector of Constabulary (HMIC), and the increasing control over the career paths of senior police officers.[8]

In the early 1980s policing in general, and the tripartite structure in particular, came under increased scrutiny. There were a number of major clashes between radical metropolitan police authorities attempting to assert control over local policing, and chief constables who, backed by the courts, successfully defended their autonomy. The Local Government Act 1985 abolished the metropolitan authorities and replaced their police committees with joint boards which consisted of councillors and magistrates nominated from the metropolitan districts. It has been suggested that the joint board police authorities have proved more accommodating to police influence than their predecessors.[9]

Police Community Consultative Groups (PCCs)

At almost the same time as these changes were being proposed and later implemented, the riots in Brixton in 1981 and a number of other inner-city areas, and the subsequent inquiry by Lord Scarman, were also focusing attention on questions of local consultation and local accountability. This led to pressures to enhance political forms of accountability within the tripartite structure. Scarman recommended that local consultative committees should be established, and statutory provision for the making of arrangements 'in each police area for obtaining the views of the people in that area about matters concerning the policing of the area and for obtaining their co-operation with the police in preventing crime in the area' were introduced under s106 of the Police and Criminal Evidence Act 1984. The form of accountability embodied in PCCs was, however, limited both in principle and practice.

The PCCs are intended to be a forum in which 'consultation' can take place. Opinions may be offered, views may be shared, and an opportunity for local representatives to influence policing policy may occur. At best, however, this is a form of 'explanatory' accountability without teeth – one in which there seems to be a general obligation on chief constables, or their representatives, to explain their actions to PCCs, but the PCCs have no sanctions to apply when explanations are considered to be unsatisfactory.

The experience of how PCCs have operated in practice rather underlines this point. Researchers[10] found that public attendance at meetings was poor, that the agenda tended to be dominated by 'police business', and that 'few PCC members have ever had adversarial contact with the police nor are they the sort of people who normally meet people who have'.

The Police and Magistrates' Courts Act 1994

Attention has now shifted somewhat away from political forms of accountability and towards financial and managerial forms. This began with the application of the government's Financial Management Initiative to the police service during the mid-1980s, which encouraged the use of business management techniques. The notion of 'contractual and managerial' accountability is a central part of the philosophy underlying the Police and Magistrates' Courts Act 1994. In practice, however, the provisions may also provide an opportunity for the enhancement of forms of political accountability.

A potentially crucial change brought in by the Act is that police authorities will be required to publish annual plans detailing local policing priorities for the coming year. These plans are to be developed in close co-operation with the chief constable, and it remains to be seen who in practice – police or local authorities – will have the greater influence. The strong opposition voiced by chief police officers to further increases in central control might make them more open to local influence, and police authorities are to be encouraged to improve and supplement existing methods of community consultation.

Opportunities for enhanced local influence may, however, be undermined by other provisions of the Act. For example, the reduction of the proportion of elected members on police authorities with the appointment of 'independent' members has been criticised as a way of ensuring compliance with the wishes of the Home Secretary (of the day). The opportunities for Home Office influence over the appointment of independent members are not clear cut, although there is evidence of 'targeting' of candidates.[11] It is possible, at least in theory, that the independent members may provide a source of expertise for the elected members.

Particular significance has been attached to the provisions in the Act that allow the Home Secretary to set national objectives and which pave the way for fixed-term contracts for senior police officers. It is feared that chief constables on such contracts will feel compelled to follow centrally-laid-down and narrowly-conceived measures of performance, rather than local needs and priorities. This is compounded by the amendment of the wording of the 1964 Act about the duty of police authorities, from providing an 'adequate and efficient' police force, to an *'effective* and efficient' one. However, some of the national objectives laid down for 1995/96 are contradictory, and far from providing a clear direction to police forces, leave considerable room for local interpretation. The nexus of control is a complicated one, and how it works in practice will, like the previous arrangements, be heavily dependent on how the relevant parties choose to use their powers.

Although the new 'financial' forms of accountability can be distinguished from political forms, it is important to note that they are not mutually exclusive – apparently neutral performance indicators can embody crucial 'political' assumptions about the nature of policing. Thus, for example, some of the current indicators reflect the narrow view of policing taken by the present Home Secretary in equating it with 'crime-fighting', for example, those encouraging increases in the number of detections for burglaries or primary 'clear-ups' of violent offences. However, despite fears about the effect of increasing emphasis on performance measurement, it has been argued that:[12]

> ...performance information might be used to generate first, improved political accountability, and second, greater responsiveness to those who use or otherwise benefit from police services.

Funding

One of the most important powers held by the Home Secretary under the 1964 Act was that of funding, with the Home Office paying 51 per cent of the police budget for each force, and exercising controls over staff complements and capital expenditure. Under the 1994 Act, each police authority will instead receive a cash limited grant from the Home Office. They will continue to receive funding from the local authorities through the revenue support grant, non-domestic rates and council tax, and s27 of the Act establishes them as precepting bodies for local government finance purposes. The chief constable and police authority, rather than the Home Secretary, will decide how to allocate funds between officers, civilian staff, vehicles, buildings and equipment. Thus, the Home Secretary will no longer specify the complement of police officers for provincial forces. These arrangements will give the police authorities and chief constables greater freedom within the budget, but the Home Secretary will have greater control over their *total spending*.

The Act also empowers the Home Secretary to instruct police authorities about measures needed to improve effectiveness and efficiency, and to lay down a minimum budget in the event of an adverse report from HMIC. The opportunities for local influence will depend upon the way in which the Home Secretary chooses to use these powers. However, the (new) arrangements do allow for a potentially greater amount of local managerial freedom within the police organisation. The codes of practice laid down under the Act encourage forces to delegate financial responsibilities to local managers which may allow for greater freedom in responding to local needs and priorities.

Legal accountability

'Accountability to the law' can operate at a number of levels, roughly corresponding to the seriousness of the case in question. Where police officers are alleged to have committed a criminal offence they may be prosecuted. The police can be sued for damages in the civil courts if it is alleged that their actions have amounted to a tort, and indeed this is an increasingly used method of redress. As a mechanism of accountability, the civil law remains an important resource in some cases, as the growing number of successful actions against the Metropolitan Police in recent years shows. Thus, both the criminal and the civil law are important sources of external accountability for the behaviour of individual police officers.

In another sense, the law holds police officers to account in the assessment of their conduct in relation to criminal cases they have constructed. The Police and Criminal Evidence Act 1984 (PACE) was intended to provide a tighter regulation of police powers. Research on the impact of PACE and the revised codes of practice has, however, been equivocal, with what appear to be some gains alongside continuing problems with regard, for example, both to suspects' rights and complaints against the police.[13] What emerges from some of the research, however, is the clear lesson that PACE and attendant codes, 'do play a crucial part in shaping the pattern of policing, but detailed provisions of the law do not influence the police in a direct and simple way'.[14]

Complaints procedures

As well taking civil action, individuals who are dissatisfied with the behaviour or the actions of the police have had recourse to a complaints procedure since the 1960s. A formal procedure for dealing with specific complaints against the police may have an important symbolic as well as an accountability function in the apparent absence of effective channels for individuals to question or influence aspects of policing.[15]

A system for dealing with all complaints against the police was introduced by the 1964 Police Act though it lacked any independent element in the investigation and adjudication of complaints. Dissatisfaction with the lack of an independent element in this procedure was widespread and almost continual, and the 1976 Police Act introduced the independent Police Complaints Board. However, this new arrangement was also never really considered satisfactory and the innovatory Police Complaints Authority (PCA) was set up in 1984 under PACE. The PCA (under s88) was allowed to supervise the investigation of 'grave' incidents referred to it by the police and a system of 'informal resolution' was introduced with the aim of conflict resolution rather than investigation and discipline. The PCA has also taken it upon itself to comment on a regular basis on certain police practices and policies.[15]

Research on the operation and 'effectiveness' of the PCA suggests that it is some distance away from working to the satisfaction of its 'users' – be they complainants or police officers.[15] First, it is doubtful whether the existence and operation of the complaints system applies sanctions in such a way as to constitute a genuine deterrent to rude or aggressive behaviour by police officers. Second, a majority of complainants were dissatisfied by the response to and outcome of their complaint, so that the PCA is currently failing in one of its key objectives

– winning public confidence. Finally, and importantly in relation to the general issue of accountability, the PCA would appear to be having little effect in improving police conduct.

External scrutiny

Since the late 1970s, there has been a significant 'opening-up' of the police service to external scrutiny, in the form of academic research,[16] audits of financial effectiveness,[17] and not least, media examinations of policing. Whilst we must accept that certain features of policing will inevitably remain hidden from public view, it is important not to underplay the significance of such developments. Perhaps most significant in terms of transparency has been the opening-up of policing to media audiences. A notable example was the BBC television 'fly on the wall' series during the early 1980s which had major implications for the way that police deal with victims of rape. Commentators have suggested '(the) decision by (the) Chief Constable of the Thames Valley Police, to allow that series of television documentaries to be made was probably more important in making police governance democratic than the whole apparatus established by the 1964 Act'.[18]

It is vital to explore ways of observing policing as it happens, as well as considering after-the-event accountability. There is need to consider accountability *during* policing, and the 'need to maximise the visibility of routine policing as it takes place'.[19]

The reforms following the Scarman report were also intended to increase the visibility of policing. Scarman had recommended that there 'should be random checks by persons other than police officers on the interrogation and detention of suspects in the police station'. There was considerable delay before the Home Office issued a Circular (12/86) which recommended the introduction of lay visiting schemes 'wherever local wishes and circumstances might make them appropriate'. Arrangements for schemes are left to individual police authorities, and their objectives are stated as:

> to enable members of the local community to observe, comment and report upon the conditions under which persons are detained at police stations and the operation in practice of the statutory and other rules governing their welfare, with a view to securing greater understanding of, and confidence in, these matters.

Internal mechanisms of accountability

Although much of the debate has concerned the establishment of effective mechanisms of external control of the police, the considerable body of research highlighting the crucial importance of internal mechanisms should not be overlooked. Indeed, one commentator places a stronger emphasis on *internal* mechanisms of accountability, largely because of the unique nature of the bulk of police work. He argues:[4]

> The primary objective to be achieved by supervisory bodies external to the police is to enhance the police organisation's capacity for effective self-regulation. Accountability can never be as effectively achieved under external auspices as it can under internal.

Achieving internal accountability for police work is significantly more difficult than for the work of many other services. This is because policing involves a major element of discretion and is low in 'visibility'. The exercise of discretion is inevitable because there are always insufficient resources to enforce all laws all the time. This applies just as much at the individual police officer level as at the force policy level. Furthermore, the work of the police officer is much less visible than that of his or her manager[20] and significantly less so than that of the chief constable. The control of officers at this level must therefore also form part of the accountability debate for, given sufficient rank-and-file autonomy, structures of accountability directed only at chief officers have little bearing on day-to-day operational policing.[21]

There are a number of ways in which the behaviour of individual police officers is internally-controlled and they are made accountable to others in (the force) for their actions. These include the occupational culture, supervision by managers to the extent that it is possible, and the police disciplinary system.

Research by the Policy Studies Institute[22] suggested that there are, in essence, three types of rule which, in varying degrees, govern police practices and that the effectiveness of each is dependent on the extent to which they are internalised. The first of these are *working rules* which are internalised by officers and 'form the guiding principles of their conduct'. In addition, there are *inhibitory rules* which are not internalised, but which are used by officers when making decisions and may, because being caught breaking them carries certain sanctions, discourage particular types of action. Finally, there are *presentational rules*, which are those which put an acceptable gloss on police practices. Given what we know about the impact of 'laws' and 'internalised rules' on police behaviour, 'the aim must be to influence the "working rules" of police culture, by changing the socialisation process and organisational rewards in appropriate ways, backed up by "inhibitory rules" but not depending on them'.[23]

Conclusions

Two very noticeable broad trends in external accountability can be identified over the past three decades which have been reinforced by the 1994 Police and Magistrates Court Act. First, there has been a move towards the concentration of power at the centre. In the main this has meant that the power of the Home Secretary, and the influence of HMIC, has increased enormously. In many, if not most, cases this expansion and concentration of power has appeared to be at the expense of local police authorities.

Second, there has been a move away from 'political' kinds of accountability, and towards 'financial' and 'managerial' modes. The increasing emphasis on financial accountability can be seen in the central role played by the activities of the Audit Commission. Managerial and financial accountability has been described as the 'contractual and calculative' mode within which performance is judged against targets which are often set centrally rather than locally and which are evaluated by HMIC. This still allows the doctrine of constabulary independence to remain apparently unchanged, whilst imposing a large variety of specific constraints on the degree to which that independence is likely to be utilised.

We have focused, like the majority of writers in the field, on external control mechanisms. Such mechanisms provide a necessary but not sufficient condition for bringing about an accountable police service. They will only be effective, however, if they are supported and complemented by highly developed internal forms of control. As Bayley[4] has argued:

> In order for processes of external regulation to succeed in the long-run, to be more than a highly publicised morality play, the police must become convinced that they will be trusted to bear most of the active responsibility for ensuring correct performance and that they have much to gain from the favourable testimony of external review agents.

References

1. Day, P. and Klein, R. (1987) *Accountabilities*. London: Tavistock.
2. Jefferson, T. and Grimshaw, R. (1984) *Controlling the Constable*. London: Frederick Muller/The Cobden Trust.
3. Reiner, R. (1993a) Police accountability: principles, patterns and practices. In Reiner, R. and Spencer, S. (eds) *Accountable Policing: Effectiveness, Empowerment and Equity*. London: Institute for Public Policy Research.
4. Bayley, D.H. (1983) Accountability and control of police: lessons for Britain. In Bennett, T. (ed) *The Future of Policing*. Cropwood Conference Series No. 15. University of Cambridge: Institute of Criminology.
5. Allen, R.J. (1976) The police and substantive rulemaking: reconciling principle and expediency. *University of Pennsylvania Law Review*, November, pp 62-117.
6. Lustgarten, L. (1986) *The Governance of Police*. London: Sweet and Maxwell.
   Smith, D.J. (1986) The framework of law and policing practice. In Benyon, J. and Bourn, C. (eds) *The Police: Powers, Procedures and Proprieties*. Oxford: Pergamon Press.
   Reiner, R. (1992) *The Politics of the Police*. (Second Edition) Hemel Hempstead: Harvester Wheatsheaf.
7. Marshall, G. (1978) Police accountability revisited. In Butler, D. and Halsey, A.H. (eds) *Policy and Politics*. London: Macmillan.
8. Reiner, R. (1992) *The Politics of the Police*. (Second Edition) Hemel Hempstead: Harvester Wheatsheaf.
9. Loveday, B. (1987) Joint boards for police in metropolitan areas – a preliminary assessment. *Local Government Studies*, 13, pp 85-101.
   Reiner, R. (1993a) Police accountability: principles, patterns and practices. In Reiner, R. and Spencer, S. (eds) *Accountable Policing: Effectiveness, Empowerment and Equity*. London: Institute for Public Policy Research.
10. Morgan, R. and Maggs, C. (1985) *Setting the PACE: Police Community Consultation Arrangements in England and Wales*. University of Bath: Centre for the Analysis of Social Policy.
    Morgan, R. (1986) Police consultative groups: the implications for the governance of the police. *Political Quarterly*, 57, pp 83-88.
    Morgan, R. (1987) The local determinants of policing policy. In Willmott, P. (ed) *Policing and the Community*. London: PSI.
    Morgan, R. (1992) Talking about policing. In Downes, D. (ed) *Unravelling Criminal Justice*. London: Macmillan.
11. Loveday, B. (1994) *Police Reform: Problems of Accountability and the Measurement of Police Effectiveness*. University of Central England: Institute of Public Policy.
12. Weatheritt, M. (1993) Measuring police performance: accounting or accountability? In Reiner, R. and Spencer, S. (eds) *Accountable Policing: Effectiveness, Empowerment and Equity*. London: Institute for Public Policy Research.
13. Brown, D. (1989) *Detention at the Police Station under the Police and Criminal Evidence Act 1984*. Home Office Research Study No. 104. London: HMSO.
    McConville, M., Sanders, A. and Leng, R. (1991) *The Case for the Prosecution*. London: Routledge.

Maguire, M. and Corbett, C. (1991) *A Study of the Police Complaints System.* London: HMSO.

14. Smith, D.J. (1986) The framework of law and policing practice. In Benyon, J. and Bourn, C. (eds) *The Police: Powers, Procedures and Proprieties.* Oxford: Pergamon Press.

15. Maguire, M. and Corbett, C. (1991) *A Study of the Police Complaints System.* London: HMSO.

16. Reiner, R. (1992) *The Politics of the Police.* Hemel Hempstead: Harvester Wheatsheaf. Second Edition.
    Hough, M. (1996) *The patrol function: what research can tell us.* In this volume.

17. Audit Commission (1990) *Effective Policing – Performance Review in Police Forces.* London: HMSO.

18. Jones, T., Newburn, T. and Smith, D.J. (1994) *Democracy and Policing.* London: Policy Studies Institute.

19. Holdaway, S. quoted in Downes, D. and Ward, T. (1986) *Democratic Policing.* London: Labour Campaign for Criminal Justice.

20. Muir, K.W. (1977) *Police: Streetcorner Politicians.* Chicago: University of Chicago Press.

21. Johnston, L. (1988) Controlling policework: problems of organisational reform in large public bureaucracies. *Work, Employment and Society,* 2, pp 51-70.

22. Smith, D.J. and Gray, J. (1985) *The Police and People in London.* Aldershot: Gower.
    Smith, D.J. (1986) The framework of law and policing practice. In Benyon, J. and Bourn, C. (eds) *The Police: Powers, Procedures and Proprieties.* Oxford: Pergamon Press.

23. Reiner, R. (1993b) Accountability and effectiveness. In Dingwall, R. and Shapland, J. (eds) *Reforming British Policing: Missions and Structures.* University of Sheffield Faculty of Law.